Courage
through the
Darkness

A JOURNEY OF HOPE AND HEALING

CYNTHIA THOMAS

WestBow
PRESS°
A DIVISION OF THOMAS NELSON
& ZONDERVAN

WestBow Press books may be ordered through booksellers or by contacting:

WestBow Press
A Division of Thomas Nelson & Zondervan
1663 Liberty Drive
Bloomington, IN 47403
www.westbowpress.com
1 (866) 928-1240

ISBN: 978-1-9736-8713-9 (sc)
ISBN: 978-1-9736-8714-6 (hc)
ISBN: 978-1-9736-8712-2 (e)

Library of Congress Control Number: 2020903938

Print information available on the last page.

WestBow Press rev. date: 03/02/2020

To those who have ever felt alone, abandoned, and afraid. For it is in our brokenness where we can find the most comfort in the arms of our loving, heavenly Father. Where He runs to meet us when we cannot seem to take a step through the darkness. Where we are unconditionally accepted and never rejected. Where we are truly loved and cherished by the very one who created us and found us worthy in His sight. Thank you, Father, for never giving up on me when I wanted to give up on life. For loving me when I could not love myself. For teaching me to persevere and triumph over adversity. For showing me how to conquer the darkness.

Contents

Acknowledgments

First, I would like to thank my amazing husband, Bret, who makes me a better person every day. Your love, patience, and support mean more to me than you will ever know. You encouraged me to share my story, one that God put down in my heart to share so very long ago. I appreciate your gentle reminders to continue writing and to keep pressing on.

Next, I would like to thank my father-in-law, Bob, who is the anchor to our family. You were the first to teach me about the love of Jesus and how to walk by faith no matter the circumstances. You are the most selfless person I know, and you have a heart for Jesus that we all strive to have. You glorify Christ in both your words and actions daily.

Furthermore, a special thank you to my sister-in-law, Theresa, who has always been my cheerleader in life. We might not be sisters by birth, but we will always be sisters by heart.

Last, I want to thank my sons, Trey and Ryan. You are my most cherished gifts from God, and I am so proud to be your mother. If not for you, I would not be here today to share my story. You kept me grounded and in the fight of life when I wanted to give up, and for that, I am so very grateful.

I love you all!

The only picture I have of myself as a young child. In it, I see
not only the little girl but the worn and battered condition of
the photo itself. Maybe this is why I have never had it repaired—
for it reminds me of how I felt much of my childhood.
Christmas 1971, age twenty-one months.

Even though I walk through the darkest valley, I will fear no evil, for you are with me; your rod and staff, they comfort me.
—Psalm 23:4

1

Broken Trust

For you created my inmost being; you knit me together in
my mother's womb. I praise you because I am fearfully and
wonderfully made; your works are wonderful, I know that full well.

—Psalm 139:13–14

I HAVE FELT A nudging from God for many years to share my personal journey of childhood abuse and trauma, but it has taken me until now to finally gain the courage to tell it. Also, I did not think that my story was anything special or worthy of being told. But I now realize that if God wants me to share it, then He will give me the courage to step out in faith, for there is a reason. If it can help just one person heal, be set free from the pain of their past, and realize they matter and are loved, then it is worth every inch of feeling vulnerable. While I desire in no way to belittle or degrade my biological family,

I have to be honest in my perception of what I faced. It is the only way healing can come forth.

This Is My Story

While I came from a humble and often turbulent beginning, God had a purpose for my very existence. In worldly standards, I was born into an impoverished and dysfunctional home without much hope of a future. It was an environment where abuse, strife, and uncertainty were around every corner, where stability did not exist. However, there is hope. The Bible says that we are fearfully and wonderfully made. God loves us unconditionally, even during the most difficult and painful times of our lives—when we cannot reciprocate His love, love ourselves, or find ourselves worthy of love in general. This is something that has taken me years to grasp. Although people may fail us, God's love never fails and can reach into the deepest, darkest hole to pull us out and place our feet on steady, solid ground, if we allow Him to.

Agape love is the highest form of love there is. It is the kind of love Jesus has for us all, the kind of love that I did not understand and lacked for so long. For agape love always protects, always trusts, always hopes, and always perseveres (1 Corinthians 13:7). This form of love is what God planned for us all from the beginning, but life and all its adversities can get in the way, causing many of us to ask the very question, "What is love?"

While the Holy Spirit gently steers us toward the ways of the Lord, He does not force us to follow the narrow path that leads to God. He gave us free will to choose our path, both the good and the bad. Unfortunately, children can become innocent bystanders of poor decisions others around them make, often leading to difficult circumstances. Although the enemy throws curveballs in life to detour us off the path of righteousness, God is faithful and just to encourage and strengthen us no matter how long it takes. He constantly pursues us!

Sometimes life's curveballs lead to broken trust, which is a tool the enemy uses to break us down, and it can prevent us from trusting anyone or anything. This is what happened to me. Due to circumstances beyond my control, the foundation of childlike faith and trust was never established, which limited my ability to fully trust the loving, heavenly Father who only wanted the best for me.

A Little about My Early Years

I was born on March 1, 1970, in a small town in Oklahoma. I am not sure my birth parents were ever married to each other, but they lived together and had four children, of which I am the oldest. Our age range is eleven months to fifteen months apart. I also have two older half sisters, one on each side and both four years older than I am. My parents had their own struggles and challenges in life without a lot of support from their families. They were products of their environment, which was not solid and lacked emotional stability. They definitely did not have a relationship with Jesus, and it showed in the everyday choices they made. That solid foundation in Christ was never developed in their own childhood years, and this limited them the rest of their lives.

While raising my own children, I often told the Lord that my heart's desire was to raise them in the "nurture and admonition of the Lord." This concept was so deeply rooted in my spirit and is something I strived to plant deep down in their hearts too. For I knew that if they were raised knowing they were loved, not only by their parents but by their heavenly Father, their foundation would not crumble when the storms of life came bearing down. They could face whatever challenge life threw at them without falling apart. Although they might stumble, they would not be overtaken. "Train up a child in the way he should go, And when he is old he will not depart from it" (Proverbs 22:6 NKJV).

This was never prayed over me, and it trickled into my adulthood, limiting my ability to fully trust and invite God into my life. While I know for a fact my parents loved me, they did not understand, nor were they taught, how to be good parents. Their internal struggles caused them to turn to alcohol—and excessive alcohol use at that. Over time, their worldly addictions took full control and made my parents choose the addictions over their own children. This is often a tool the enemy uses to divide families and tear them apart.

A Little about My Biological Parents

My father had nineteen brothers and sisters, many of whom he never even met before he died from a heart attack at the age of fifty. His father was married twice and had ten children with each marriage. Only recently have I begun to reconnect with family on my father's side, and I am slowly learning more about his side of the family. One of his sisters actually raised him. He was one of the youngest of his siblings, and I have often thought about how lonely and rejected he must have felt growing up without his father in his life, causing him to falter in his responsibility as a father to his own children. We tend to parent as we were parented unless the unhealthy cycle is broken. I have no doubt the Holy Spirit teaches us how to parent if we allow Him to. Jesus said, "But the Advocate, the Holy Spirit, whom the Father will send in my name, will teach you all things and will remind you of everything I have said to you" (John 14:26). Therefore, all we have to do is ask, and we shall receive. It is that simple.

I reconnected with my father when I was sixteen and saw firsthand the two sides of him: a deeply shy and soft-spoken man with a kind heart when sober and the loud, obnoxious, angry man when drinking. His entire demeanor changed when alcohol consumed him. He was almost demon-like in his actions and behavior. It shows that if we give the enemy an inch into our lives, he will take a mile!

Overall, when I think about my father, tears flow. I feel so much grief and emotion that even to this day I do not fully understand. I am not sure if it is the little girl inside who strongly desires a connection with her earthly father, or if there are buried memories of actual good times she had with him in her younger years. I miss him every day and just hope one day we meet again in heaven. To see him the way God created him to be would be amazing! There are many times that I actually cry when watching a father with his daughter, something I wish I could have experienced here on earth. I have been blessed with an amazing father-in-law who calls me "daughter." This touches my heart in so many ways. He was the first man to actually teach me about the love of Christ, and he demonstrates daily how to walk in love. I have no doubt that God put this man in my life to show me genuine fatherly love, and for this I am so very grateful.

However, to be honest, it just is not the same as one's own biological father loving his little girl and striving to protect her from the challenges of the world. I have often watched my oldest son with his daughters, and I see pure love and joy in his eyes when he looks at them. The way he encourages them, hugs them, plays with them, teaches them, and comforts them is so very special to see. I believe

God wanted me to witness this special bond between a father and his little girl to show me how magnificent He designed it to be. It was not the painful and broken life I lived every day in my young years. Instead, this is how our heavenly Father wants an earthly father to love his children—with agape love.

For a short time in my early twenties, I lived with my father and one of his sisters. I remember just loving being in the same room as he was. He enjoyed watching old westerns on TV. He had some health issues that caused chronic pain. He was wheelchair bound due to losing his right lower leg and the tips of several fingers. My heart hurts thinking about how much pain he was in physically. But I never heard him complain about it. Instead, he suffered quietly and turned to alcohol as a way of coping with the stressors he faced, physically and emotionally. I grieve knowing he did not know Jesus, because if he had at the time, he would have had a peace that would have surpassed all understanding. He would have realized he truly was loved and not forgotten and left to suffer alone. For he would have experienced sustaining grace. I know Jesus was there with him since He promises to never leave us or forsake us, but my father did not receive Him in his heart, limiting Jesus's ability to move in his life. This is why it is so important to allow Christ to walk with us, and even carry us at times, during struggles and difficulties we face. "The Lord is close to the brokenhearted and saves those who are crushed in spirit" (Psalm 34:18).

When I lived with him, I was in nursing school, and I would sit in the living room doing my homework just to be near him. I often caught him staring at me for no reason. I asked him why he stared, and he told me he saw my mother in me. I have no doubt he loved my mother and his children, but he was unable to defeat his internal demons; they had a strong grip on him and suffocated him to his very core. During one conversation, he told me how sorry he was for abandoning my siblings and me during our childhood. We both wept. He asked for forgiveness, and it was amazing how quickly I forgave him.

While I have a softness in my heart for my father, this has not always been the case for my biological mother, and I am not sure exactly why. My mother had one sister and four brothers. She never graduated from high school, and she had her first child at age eighteen. When thinking of my mother, anger was always the predominant emotion that surfaced. While I do not remember everything from my childhood, something happened to trigger such a strong response on my part. I guess some of it stems from being a mother myself. Mothers are supposed to nurture and protect their children, two things that she did not do for her own. Years ago, the Lord told me, "You are a lot like your mother." I am not going to lie. This angered me to my core! I told the Lord that I was *nothing* like my mother. While still fuming in my heart, I heard that still, small voice say, "You are like the person I created her to be." In that conversation, I saw firsthand how God has a plan for our lives, but life, circumstances, environment, and sin can cause us to veer off course and go onto a destructive, painful path, one that God never planned for us to journey down. However, with faith and trust, we can steer once again onto the right path, with the still, small voice leading the way. It is never too late to turn around. For He desires to give us hope and a prosperous future (see Jeremiah 29:11). This is His promise to us, if only we grasp it and hold on.

Many years ago, the adoption agency sent me a summary of health and family history. It stated that I had been seen for medical conditions such as head lice, skin infections, and anemia on more than one occasion before adoption. In addition, it showed that at the age of five, I was referred to an orthopedist for a questionable unhealed clavicle fracture. The orthopedist stated that I was probably born with a malformed clavicle. This was alarming to me, as apparently my biological parents were unaware that I had a malformed clavicle since birth. I knew every little detail about my children, so I could not fathom how any parent did not know their child well enough.

The summary further outlined a quote from one of the DHS social workers when talking about my mother. It stated, "She is handicapped by ignorance, poverty, and the bitterness of unhappiness experienced in life." However, it further stated that her manner of speaking about devotion for her children appeared entirely sincere. I have no doubt this was the case and that she loved her children immensely. But her internal struggles dominated and caused her to make inadequate choices in life, with her children ultimately suffering the consequences.

Many years ago, God gave me a dream of Him sitting in a rocking chair, holding me over His shoulder, rocking me as a grown woman, telling me He was nurturing me the way my mother never did. This stirred such compassion and a sense of belonging in my heart. In an unexplained way, it caused me to see my own mother in a different light, one where I felt sorry for her, since I do not believe she ever experienced such joy as this while here on earth. He is indeed a Father to the fatherless. He was encouraging me to allow Him to demonstrate a parental love like I had never experienced before, the agape love that He aspired for my earthly parents to show me but that they never could.

"Can a mother forget the baby at her breast and have no compassion on the child she has borne? Though she may forget, I will not forget you! See, I have engraved you on the palms of my hands; your walls are ever before me."

—Isaiah 49:15–16

2

❦

Fear of the Dark

For God has not given us a spirit of fear, but of
power and of love and of a sound mind.

—2 Timothy 1:7 (NKJV)

THE MAJORITY OF my childhood memories include being removed from my home and taken to different shelters and foster homes before I was adopted at the age of eight. One particular time, a DHS worker showed up late at night to take us to what looked like a library, after we were found to be alone in our home. There were books everywhere. My three younger siblings and I slept on a rollaway bed all huddled together, trying to comfort one another through the night. Sadly, incidents like this became a way of life for us due to the instability of our home environment.

I have several vivid memories of my time in foster care, and there are two particular homes I remember quite fondly. The first one was with a couple who lived on a farm not far from my birth town. I remember riding on a combine during wheat harvest and chasing rabbits in the fields. One time I went to the local pool and saw one of my sisters there. I was so happy and excited to see her. She had been placed in a different foster home, but somehow we were able to be together, even if for just a short time. However, I was not at this home for very long before being returned to my birth parents once again.

My favorite foster home was with a nice couple in Oklahoma. They owned a local hardware store in a small town. There was another girl in the home, also around my age. I believe I was around seven years old at the time. Joy and happiness shone all around me during my days with them. Ironically, I was particularly drawn to my foster father. He was kind and loving toward me. However, I still remember not letting my guard down with him. It was too painful to let anyone in, even someone I had connected with and grown very fond of. I was suddenly removed from their home after they told the DHS social worker they wanted to adopt me. For whatever reason, this was not an option for them. I was heartbroken, to say the least. Just as I was getting comfortable and feeling safe in their home, I was once again uprooted and returned to my biological parents. In the late nineties, I was fortunate to reconnect with my favorite foster parents. When we met again after all those years, my foster father gave me a children's book about being special in spite of what others says or think about you, for we are special to our Creator. He did not sign his name inside the book. Instead, he wrote that it was from "someone who knows how special you are." This touched me deeply since it showed how much he had cared for me. For so many years, I did not feel special at all to anyone. This one simple gesture touches my heart even to this day. I still have this book, and I have read it to my granddaughters to help them understand just how special they are not only to me but also to God.

I can count on one hand the number of good memories of my early years. Instead, my memories often consist of difficult times where I felt abandoned and fearful. Fear was the dominant emotion that controlled me as a child. The enemy knew the calling I had on my life and threw out different obstacles to try to stop God moving in my life. This is how the enemy works. He attacks us during our most vulnerable, weakest times. This is often during our formative childhood years, where he can cause strongholds to become rooted that very often continue into our adulthood. The root of fear was so deeply engrained into every part of my being. I was scared of everything. As a child, I was told that the devil would grab my feet while I slept, so I slept in a fetal position with my legs drawn to my chest, hoping nothing would grab me in the dark. I was told that he would reach up and grab me as I sat on the toilet. Can you imagine how it felt to be scared to even sit on the toilet? Also, I was told that he would grab me from under the bed as I walked by. For years, I had to look under the bed to make sure nothing was there. I was constantly on guard, trying to protect myself any way I knew how, often from an unknown predator.

I had to sleep with someone else in the room, as I was too afraid to sleep alone. It could be a person or an animal; I just did not want to be alone. It was the only way I could relax enough to sleep well. I never slept alone until age forty. Yes, age forty! Fear was a way of life for me, and darkness triggered the fear that consumed me. I was locked in closets as a young child, dragged from my bed, and

13

beaten during the night for unknown reasons. So, it is easy to see how the enemy planted fear as a deep root in my soul that would take years and lots of trust and faith to uproot. But thankfully, God had a plan.

As I got older and started reading the Bible, a scripture that I repeated over and over at night to help me combat the fear of the dark was "In peace I will lie down and sleep, for you alone, Lord, make me dwell in safety" (Psalm 4:8). While my heart wanted to believe God would keep me safe as I slept, my mind often told me something different. The battlefield is in the mind, and the key to healing is changing how we think. We have to cast down any thought that is not of God (see 2 Corinthians 10:5 NKJV). This allows us to take control of what we are thinking, for this is how we win the battle in the mind.

I do believe that the spirt of fear was a generational curse that stemmed from many generations before me on both sides of my family. It was one that had to be broken for the sake of my children and grandchildren. Romans 12 talks about the need to renew the mind. God knew that in order to be fully set free, I had to renew how I thought about things. While the enemy had used people over the years to engrain fear into every fiber of my soul, causing me to constantly worry about everything, the Bible is a road map to help us know how to overcome strongholds the enemy sets in our lives. For "the weapons we fight with are not the weapons of the world. On the contrary, they have divine power to demolish strongholds" (2 Corinthians 10:4).

To help accomplish this when I am afraid, I now say to myself, "I am courageous and calm in any situation. I am strong in Christ." Although I may be shaking and trembling while saying these words, it is imperative I face the challenge before me to not allow the fear to consume me. God promises to never leave us or forsake us, so I must *believe* that He is there with me, no matter what I am facing. When traumatic experiences occur in our lives, the limbic system in the brain kicks into overdrive to protect us. We can get stuck in a patterned response. Therefore, each time we are exposed to a past trigger of fear, anxiety and panic can occur. This is why the mind *must* be renewed in order to transition the negative response toward a more positive response.

The last house I remember living in before being adopted was a tiny two-bedroom house on Littel Street in my birth hometown. It sat in front of a railroad track where homeless people often stayed. On several occasions, I remember hiding in my bedroom closet while intruders tried to break in when no adults were home. With no comfort and support from my parents, fear took hold once again.

Another incident occurred when I was hospitalized at the age of three for what I found out later to be a severe case of Salmonella, from which I almost died. While I was too young to know why I was hospitalized, my adoption records provided details surrounding this traumatic experience that I still recall so vividly. I remember being in a room with a crib and TV across the room. A lady, who I assume to be a nurse, came in and literally tied me down in four-point restraints for IV therapy. I cried and cried with no parent or other known family member present to comfort me. Afterward, the lady untied me, gave me some ice cream, and turned the TV to cartoons. To this day, I hate being restrained in any form. It causes me to feel panicky. This is something God is still working on with me. It is a constant battle.

One time when my sons were little, they put toy handcuffs on me. I began panicking and broke the handcuffs into pieces. After the incident, they showed me there was a button that could have been pushed to release the handcuffs, but panic had instantly set in. The look on my sons' faces was pure sadness. I felt awful for breaking their toy! However, that traumatic event thirty-plus years before still haunted me and showed in my behavior that day. That trigger was real, and it caused me to lose all sense of reality in that moment. Interestingly, I never had this as a trigger until God started healing me in my late twenties. I had always remembered the event, but I had not felt the emotion associated with it before then. I assume it was because that painful, traumatic experience had been buried so deeply in such a secure place down in my soul that I had never allowed it to be revealed to anyone, including myself. I was in survival mode, and it was much too painful to allow that box to be opened. It was how I coped as a child and was able to face the challenges I endured. I believe God allowed me to place that pain there for a season. He knew that one day it would be safe to open that box and allow that deeply rooted pain to surface, in order to be set free and healed from it. It had to come out of darkness and into the light. For He came to set the captives free, and I was a wounded girl who needed a freedom that only God could give.

While there were many painful and fearful memories in that tiny house, there were also a few good times. One in particular consisted of lying in front of our old TV, watching a kids' show and laughing. My siblings and I had a large bowl of cereal, and we all had our own spoons and were digging in. From what I remember, no adults were in the house. All we had was one another—my brother, my two sisters, and me. And in that moment, all was well. Laughter and joy overpowered the fear and turmoil, even if just for a short time. Eventually though, the good memories would be pushed out by the traumatic ones that eventually led my siblings and me into the DHS system one final time.

I was molested on several occasions during my younger years, and it left a deep wound in my soul. It took me years to forgive my offenders and to forgive myself for allowing it to happen, although I know I was a helpless child who had no control over the situation. I guess I was angry at myself for never telling anyone about the incidents.

Probably the most painful and difficult childhood memory stems from when I was molested around the age of seven. This was one of multiple times over my young years but definitely one that I remember in the greatest detail. I was lying on our lower bunk bed beside one of my siblings (I am not sure which one). My other two siblings were asleep on the top bunk. Rarely, my mother had a babysitter watch us. Usually, we were just left alone. However, this particular day, she got a teen male, who I did not know, to watch us. During my sleep, I was startled awake by this male lying on top of me, fondling me. I felt something sticky on my abdomen that, looking back, was probably semen. I remember reaching over with my left hand to my sibling and holding their hand for comfort. I quietly sobbed. After the incident, he threatened to hurt me if I told anyone, so I kept quiet. A few days later, one of my uncles took me into my mother's room and asked me what was wrong. He said he had noticed I was quieter than usual. I did not tell him about what happened to me that long, painful night. I never told anyone about the incident until I was an adult and only as I began to heal. To be honest, I was very angry at God for many years over the abuse I suffered as a child. Why did He not stop it when He could have? Why me? What did I do to deserve this? Why could I not have had a normal childhood? However, in time, God gave me the answer.

About twenty years ago, I had a dream where I was back in that bunk bed, facing that awful situation again around the age of seven. The difference was that, in my dream, someone was holding my right hand this time. When I looked over, I saw Jesus standing there weeping with me. He said, "While your parents usurped their God-given protection over you in the spiritual realm, it allowed the enemy to attack you. However, you are a grown woman now, and you can choose my protection, and I will restore you." I then woke up. To be honest, I had to look up the definition of "usurped" since I did not know what it meant. In this dream, He showed me that He anguished over what happened to me. I was in that situation due to the poor decisions my parents made, for they had free will. I was an innocent bystander in it all, but He knew one day I would make decisions for myself, and I could *choose* a healthier path for my future. It is amazing how the Holy Spirit works! This dream was very freeing to me. It opened my eyes to the fact that Jesus was there the entire time, and He never left me or forsook me during the deepest, darkest times of my life—times when I felt alone, abandoned, and rejected by the very ones who were supposed to be shielding and protecting me. It was only after this that I was able to start stepping out in faith and on my journey to healing from my past. I was learning to trust someone for the first time in my life. I started with baby steps, and I am still learning to take leaps of faith, with God holding my hand the entire way. For He promises to never leave us or forsake us.

Because God has said, "Never will I leave
you; never will I forsake you."
—Hebrews 13:5

3

❦

Persevering through Pain

Blessed is the one who perseveres under trial because,
having stood the test, that person will receive the crown of
life that the Lord has promised to those who love him.
—James 1:12

ONE OF MY strongest memories is from the age of seven when
we were removed from our home by the DHS system for the last
time. I remember my mother speaking with someone on the phone,
telling them, "Come get them. I don't want them anymore." A short
time later, a brown car pulled into the driveway, and a man was
there to pick us up. While this had happened many times before,
even at my young age, I felt this time was different, and I was right.
In the past, my mother would cry and beg for them to not take us
away. This time, she had asked them to. She told us to get into the

vehicle. She just handed us over without guilt or remorse. While I was helping my brother and youngest sister into the vehicle, my six-year-old sister stood hugging the porch pole. My mother told her to get into the vehicle, and she turned and spit right into my mother's face. So much anger and resentment was displayed in that moment. I still remember that all these years later. We never returned to that little house again. A year later, I was adopted and separated from my siblings, who had always been my rock and comfort. This caused walls to develop around me, a type of shell to keep all the pain out so that nothing could hurt me ever again. I learned to depend on me and me alone. To that point, every adult in my life had failed me.

March 17, 1978, was the day I was adopted into a new family who lived only about eighty miles from my birth hometown. I was eight years old. At that time, I was an only child. Four years later, I would get a brother, my adopted parents' first and only biological child. I was a timid girl and very much an introvert by nature. I enjoyed quietness and fell apart with yelling and strife, so in the beginning, I welcomed my new environment since I found it to be peaceful and inviting. I enjoyed playing with my Baby Alive doll and spending time doing arts and crafts. I took piano lessons, joined Brownies, and played soccer. My adopted parents exposed me to a life that I had never seen before, and at first, I reveled in it.

I was tough and very much a tomboy, but interestingly, I despised getting dirty, especially my hands. I also hated taking baths as a child. I suspect this was partly due to the lack of bathing in my years before adoption. According to my adoption records, I often lived with biological family members who did not have working utilities in the home. The report documented how poor the living conditions were and that we were unclean and neglected. Sadly, I had suffered from multiple types of abuse: physical, emotional, sexual, and neglect.

However, some of my fondest childhood memories are of my adopted grandparents' farm in Arkansas. From age eight to age sixteen, I spent quite a few summers there, and I felt free and alive! In addition to my foster father, I developed a soft spot in my heart for my adopted grandfather. He was such a strong but gentle man— different from others. I saw qualities in him that I had not seen in other men, and it drew me to him. I loved him deeply.

The farm animals quickly became my friends, and I enjoyed farm life. I helped my grandmother work in the garden. We picked vegetables for our meals, and I particularly enjoyed learning to snap green beans. I helped feed cattle and rode horses. I especially enjoyed fishing with my grandfather. They even allowed one of their dogs to sleep with me, which was so comforting. When my sons were in grade school, we went and visited my grandmother one last time on the farm before she sold it after my grandfather had passed away. To see my children playing much like I did as a little girl was very special. Witnessing the innocence and joy of childhood through their eyes was priceless. I will always cherish my memories of that peaceful farm. Looking back, I see how God allowed me to have these experiences to help drown out some of the painful memories of my earlier years. I am so thankful my children got to experience it too.

My adopted parents were well educated and very loving people. They provided me with a safe and wonderful life. However, something prevented me from being able to fully engage with them and enjoy my new stable home to the fullest. I just could not seem to lower the walls of steel I had placed around me. It seemed so foreign to me. No chaos or turmoil. Instead, just a calm, inviting environment that seemed so backward to this wounded little girl. In the beginning, I thrived, but the older I got, the more I craved my prior turbulent life and longed to be back there with my siblings, whom I missed fiercely.

I had no idea where they were or if I would ever see them again, and this angered me to my core, especially the older I got. While life went on around me, I slowly withdrew from everyone and everything. This became worse the closer I got to my teen years, where rebellion set in. One could say I was a rebellious teenager. My strong will and determination helped me survive a difficult home environment as a young child. However, it limited my ability to positively grow and change as a teenager. Anger toward my adoptive parents grew more and more over time. I never felt connected to them from the start, often feeling like the black sheep of the family. However, they never did anything to cause me to feel this way. Instead, they loved me unconditionally and welcomed me with open arms as a parent should, but I was never able to accept their love or allow myself to connect with them in a productive way. I always called my adoptive mother "mom," but I called my adoptive dad by his first name and never "dad." He never did anything wrong though. I just never felt a connection with him. I found it difficult to allow myself to get close to males in general, because of how men had treated me in the past. My view of men was skewed and downright repulsive, to be honest.

I went to a private Catholic high school after attending public school for my elementary years, where I was in gifted and talented classes. While I certainly had the ability to do well in high school, I intentionally did not turn in homework or put forth any real effort. My teachers saw potential in me and recommended I enroll in honors courses to prepare for college, but I refused to participate. I just did not seem to care about anything, and I had no real drive to succeed. I was spiraling down a dark path and picking up speed. My adopted parents saw my struggle and sent me to a child psychologist when I was fourteen years old. I intentionally did not engage in any conversation and just sat listening to my Walkman during the visits. I did not care to listen to anything he had to say. This behavior continued session after session until he finally told them that I was the second most oppositional child he had ever dealt with in his entire practice and that he could not help me. He told my adopted parents, "She will either use this to her benefit or her demise. The ball is in her court." After that, they placed me in a girls' home in another city in Oklahoma, at the age of fourteen. I was so angry, which intensified my rebellion even more. After several months of being there, I ran away from the home with another girl. We hitchhiked with a truck driver so I could attend a basketball game at the Catholic high school I had attended prior. I stayed at the home of one of my friends from school and hid out in her bedroom until the police found me and took me back to my adopted parents' home. I am so very thankful that God protected us that day. My heart wrenches just thinking about what could have happened to my friend or me. The very next day, my adopted parents returned me to the girls' home.

While there, I saw a psychologist who told me that I had a cocoon built around me and that I would not allow the beautiful butterfly to be released. I did not understand what he meant at the time, nor did I even care. However, I believe God used him and others to plant seeds along the way to encourage me to let my guard down and allow the heavenly Father to transform me into the person He designed me to be, instead of the person the world was trying to mold me into. I remember feeling so unworthy and downright disgusting during my teen years. I often wore baggy clothes to hide my figure. I guess I felt this was safe at the time—a way of hiding from the world in order to not have attention focused on me. I always felt I belonged at the end of the line and never at the front, for I felt unworthy.

I fully believe my nine months in the girls' home was a crossroads for me. It is where I accepted Jesus Christ as my Lord and Savior and where I found acceptance and love on a different level than ever before. Sharon P. worked at the girls' home and was a woman God used to change my life forever. I called her Ms. P., and I was especially drawn to her and did anything she asked me to do, without question. I thought she was cool since she was from California and wore flip-flops. I have no doubt God orchestrated everything and used her to fulfill His plan of reaching me. I believe we will all come to a crossroads at some point in our lives, and this was mine. For it is where I found what was missing in my life all along. It was a crossroads where I had to make a choice to either serve God or serve the world. Jesus said, "Enter through the narrow gate. For wide is the gate and broad is the road that leads to destruction, and many enter through it. But small is the gate and narrow the road that leads to life, and only a few find it" (Matthew 7:13–14).

Sharon P. asked me one day if I had ever accepted Jesus into my heart. I had no idea what she was talking about and told her no. She said, "When you are lying in your bed tonight, ask Jesus to come into your heart, and your life will never be the same again. But remember, do not put God in a box. He is so much bigger than you can ever imagine." I remember her every word to this day. Well, I did as she said. I lay in my bed and asked Jesus into my heart that very night. The next day, I felt a peaceful presence over my right shoulder like I had never felt before. I kept turning around, looking behind me. It was as if something or someone was there with me that I could not see. That one act of obedience changed my life forever. I have no doubt that my life would be completely different, and not in a good way, if I had not made the decision that day to follow the narrow road that Christ had placed before me. Although challenges still came even after making this decision, it gave God permission to come into my life, where He gently nudged and encouraged me to not wander off the narrow road even when roadblocks came.

After accepting Jesus, I heard the song "Bridge over Troubled

Water,"[1] and I felt as if God had given me the song as a promise to me. I clung to it. The part in the song that says "Sail on silver girl, sail on by, your time has come to shine, all your dreams are on their way, see how they shine" resonated with me, and it still does to this day. God often reminds me of that promise He gave to me all those years ago when I face challenging times. He was showing me that it was time to shine and come out of the darkness, for now I was safe. So, I have learned to cling to His promises, no matter how bleak life may look. He is the same yesterday, today, and forever. He changes not. What He promised yesterday is still true today. As far as Sharon P., I hope one day I can hug her in heaven and thank her for what she did for me. It was truly life changing.

God used others to teach me to be persevere through the pain and to never give up, even though it seemed hopeless and desolate at the time. He was teaching me to be an overcomer and to know that He never left me or abandoned me. He was teaching me that my best days were yet to come. All I had to do was hold on, *trust*, and enjoy the ride, for difficult journeys often lead to beautiful destinations.

When I am afraid, I put my trust in you.
—Psalm 56:3

4

ᑲ

Finding Courage

Have I not commanded you? Be strong and courageous.
Do not be afraid; do not be discouraged, for the Lord
your God will be with you wherever you go.
—Joshua 1:9

COURAGE IS HAVING the ability to do something that
frightens you.[1] It is being steadfast and facing something that normally
would cause one to turn and run—and instead moving forward, even
if shaking and trembling. It is more or less doing it afraid. Courage
is not doing something in the absence of fear; it is doing something
in spite of fear. I believe John Wayne said it best: "Courage is being
scared to death, but saddling up anyway."[2]

Over the years, I have often thought about how it would feel to be
courageous since I seemed to lack it all the way around. I was a shy

girl who adamantly avoided confrontation at all costs, and I would literally fall apart and retreat back to a perceived safe place when exposed to it. I despised any attention on myself and preferred to hide in the shadows of others. This followed me even into my adult years, often limiting my ability to pursue certain jobs in nursing, due to fear of public speaking. While I am certain some of this is just my personality, I do believe that the trauma I faced intensified my struggle. Boldness definitely was not an attribute I manifested. Strangely enough, in my early teen years, I found solace in my bedroom closet, often locking myself in there, away from the troubles of the world. A closet was often a place of fear and torment for me as a young child, but somehow it also became a kind of safe haven too.

Looking back over the years, I see how I had more courage than I thought. For a young, abused child to have survived what I went through and to be where I am today, it most certainly took courage—God-given courage and strength. Courage to survive kept me in the fight. God commands us to fear not, to be of good cheer, and to have courage. He wants us to launch out into the deep waters with the knowledge and belief that He will guide us safely to shore. He is the beacon of light in the storm to show us the way. Psalm 119:105 says, "Your word is a lamp for my feet, a light on my path."

One of my favorite paintings that I have is of a man standing in the doorway of a lighthouse in the middle of the rough sea. Angry waves swirled all around him, but he was not fazed by what he saw. I believe that he understood and fully trusted in God's promise to protect him from the storm that was bearing down on him. What courage that took! His stance fully demonstrated what the Bible instructs us to do: "For we walk by faith, not by sight" (2 Corinthians 5:7 NKJV). He trusted in spite of what he saw with his eyes. Instead of looking at the storm upon him, he chose to look at the one who created the universe, the one who is sovereign and always faithful.

Oh, to trust like that! This has been a challenging concept for me over the years, one that I am still striving to conquer.

As I have walked through my journey, the Lord has shown me that it actually took courage to walk away intact from the horrific environment I faced as a young child. Fear, rejection, and anxiety were everyday emotions that I felt. They were comfortable and familiar, no matter how odd that sounds, for it was all I knew. I learned to adapt to situations by using the strong will that God gave me to survive. Being strong willed kept me in the fight and allowed me to keep pressing on and to not give up. For if I gave in, this world would have consumed me early on.

Although I was in a healthier environment after adoption, I felt like an outsider looking in. This only intensified when my younger brother was born. As previously stated, my adopted parents were nothing but loving, accepting, and genuine to me. It was I who could not accept their love and allow my wounded heart to heal. It would be many years before I allowed my heart of stone to become a heart of flesh.

One of my fond memories is of making homemade cherry pies with my adopted mother when I was about ten years old. I always looked forward to making them for the holidays. However, I worked really hard to make them perfect, and I would become frustrated if they did not measure up to my high standards. I would measure the width of the lattice crust to assure each strip was the same size. I was hard on myself, much harder than anyone else could be. Anything less than perfect was not an option. It was how I measured my worth.

Over the years, I have learned to see lessons and even beauty in mistakes. I am no longer afraid to let people see my flaws or to be the real me. For so long, I hid my imperfections and scars. However, I realized that life is messy and oftentimes unpredictable. We must not fall apart or blame ourselves for things we have no control over. Even

Jesus chose to display his scars as a reminder of His faithfulness and love for us all, even though we sent Him to the cross. Our scars are evidence of healing and saying, "I am a survivor." It is through our pain and the scars of life that greatness can prevail—greatness that brings glory not to ourselves but to God. Scars display God's mercy in allowing us to overcome and be healed from wounds that easily could have overtaken us if we allowed them to.

I believe that God uses our deepest sorrows and pain to develop our greatest testimony. It is in the fire where courage and steadfast determination develop. It is where we see that in our weakness, we are made strong. I read something recently that said, "Remember Shadrach, Meshach and Abednego? God didn't put out the fire, He just put Jesus in there with them. It is not about God 'putting out our fire,' it is about Who is there with you" (author unknown). With God's help, I have no doubt that one day I will stand victorious over my past failures and, once and for all, triumph over what the enemy planned for my demise. I just have to remember who I belong to, rise up, take courage, and do it!

Rise up … take courage and do it.
—Ezra 10:4

5

Searching for Truth

Children are a heritage from the Lord,
offspring a reward from him.

—Psalm 127:3

WHEN I WAS sixteen, I set out to locate my biological parents. I was determined to find them. I had this fantasy that everything would be better if I could just return to my roots. I remembered that my grandmother had owned a bar in my birth hometown. I had vivid memories of my siblings and me sleeping in the back of a bar. Therefore, I started my search by calling every bar in my hometown until I reached someone who knew my biological parents. On my second attempt, a lady answered the phone, and I asked for my birth parents by name. Amazingly, I was speaking with my maternal aunt. She initially thought I was a bill collector, but she soon found out it was me. She said, "Well, Cindy, this is your aunt you're speaking to." She told me she would contact my mother and have her call me right back. At the time, my mother lived with her oldest brother in another town. I nervously waited for the phone to ring. It was extremely difficult for me to make conversation, so panic was already setting in. I had no idea what I would say when she called or if I would even be able to speak at all. However, I regained my composure and answered the phone when it rang.

My mother and I spoke for a short time before making arrangements to meet that following weekend in my birth hometown, where the majority of my biological family still resided. My adopted mother was gracious and drove me the eighty miles to meet them. She bought me a disposable camera, so I could take a lot of pictures. I never appreciated how incredibly difficult that must have been for her until I became a mother myself. The love she must have had for me! It brings tears to my eyes to think about it now. I will always be grateful for her act of kindness, one that I am not sure I could have shown if I had been in her situation. I have no doubt God's grace sustained her that day.

When we turned down the street, I saw a large group of people standing in the front yard of the address we were given. I immediately slid onto the floorboard of the passenger seat out of pure terror. My heart was racing. I hated attention on myself, so this certainly was uncomfortable for me. My adopted mother pulled into the driveway. I cautiously opened the door, and while trying to get out, I felt someone reach out, grab me, and hug me with the tightest hug. It was my biological mother, and she was crying. Off in the distance was my biological father, standing in the background, as I later found out he often did. I find myself much like him in many ways. I too wanted to be standing in the background away from all of the focus I was being given, much like a typical introvert.

After introductions, my adopted mother helped me unload my overnight bag, and she made sure I had money and my bus ticket to return home in two days. She gave me a final hug and drove away. I cannot tell you every feeling that I felt in that moment, but I do know that I felt like I belonged for the first time in a very long time. How odd that must sound, but oh so true! Although I had not been born into the best home environment, in that moment, I felt a strange sense of peace and acceptance. I immediately sensed that these were my people. I cannot explain it, but I just knew. They presented pictures of me as a young child. This was so amazing, since I never had any pictures before the age of eight. To see that I resembled some of those around me was so exciting. They had remembered me and had not forgotten me!

Later that day, one of my uncles told me that he was surprised I was the first one to find them since I acted "prissy" as a child. He thought I would find a good home and never look back. While this seemed like the way to go, I firmly believe that it was God's desire and will for me to return to my roots in order to be set free from the bondage of my past. Only by facing it would I be able to overcome it.

After I returned to my adopted parents' home, I rebelled even more. I sank further into despair and depression. I longed for my biological family and wanted to be with them. Therefore, I called my biological maternal grandmother and asked if I could live with her. She agreed to adopt me back into the family, and my adopted parents graciously honored my request. I feel deep down that they knew that they had to let me go, no matter how difficult it was for them. I made the choice to give up the life I had been living for the past eight years—a life that any child would be blessed to have. At the time, I could not see it for what it was. I found out years later that neither my biological mother nor father could petition to adopt me back into the family since their parental rights were terminated when they failed to show up for court to fight for me all those years ago.

The day of the adoption hearing, I walked into the bathroom at the courthouse and saw my adopted mother standing there crying. I just stood there. I remember feeling emotionless and unsympathetic to how she was feeling. It tears my heart out to think about it now. I am ashamed of how heartless I was. I have since asked for forgiveness for my lack of empathy toward her. I am truly grateful for everything my adopted parents did for me. They exposed me to a different way of life than what I was born into. They taught me that the sky was the limit and I was the only one who could stop me. They taught me that with determination and hard work, I could do anything I put my mind to, that I had potential—if only I would tap into it and believe.

At one point, my adopted mother told me that they had no idea about the abuse I had suffered. She said the social worker failed to disclose this very important information when they were trying to adopt me. I wondered if that would have made a difference in their decision to proceed with the adoption. Nonetheless, I am grateful they chose me, for they most certainly did not have to. They only wanted a child to love and call their own. Instead, they got a deeply wounded and damaged little girl who had built a cocoon around herself and refused to let them in. I am so thankful God gave them a biological child after they struggled to have one for so many years. At least they had another child to love, one who could reciprocate their love on a level they deserved, the parent/child bond of love.

Well, I found out very quickly that things were not peaches and cream back in my birth hometown. I saw firsthand my biological parents' dysfunction and emotional struggles. Lack of adequate coping skills leading to substance abuse controlled their decisions and very way of life. How could they fully love me when they could not even love themselves? For one cannot give something they do not have. I found myself constantly looking for my father in the local bars or on the riverbanks, where I often found him drinking with his buddies. I wanted to know he was safe, even if I just observed it from a distance. I knew never to approach him when he was drinking, for this triggered a deeply rooted fear in me. I still have flashbacks of times he beat my mother in the little house so many years before. I would hide when he came in after a long night of drinking. Oddly, the dark became a place where I could hide away in the shadows to go unnoticed, but it was also a place of much pain and fear.

I lived with my maternal grandmother initially but soon found myself being tossed around between extended family members. I went to the local public school but never really connected with anyone. I was very much a loaner and preferred privacy over socializing. I played hooky at school quite often and found myself in the principal's office on more than one occasion. I felt a lack of control over my situation that only intensified over time. Strangely enough, I longed to be back at my adopted parents' home, but I was too proud to reach out to them. I had been fortunate enough to have tasted the better life with my adopted parents, so I knew there was something more out there in the world than what I was being shown at that moment. I just needed a way to get there and to get out.

Looking back, I have no doubt that I was indeed on the path I needed to be on in order to move forward in life and to once and for all allow that painful sore to finally scab over. It was a way to allow the chains of my past to be released once and for all so that complete healing could come forth. I yearned to fill the void I felt of being parentless here on earth. While my adopted parents were wonderful people, they just were not *my people.* I needed to have a sense of feeling wanted and not just someone tossed away by the very ones who gave me life. I needed to meet them again so I could move beyond seeing them through rose-colored glasses and be forced to look at their flaws. In some crazy way, I blamed myself for my birth parents giving me up so easily. Surely, I had caused it. Maybe I was not good enough, strong enough, or helpful enough. There had to be a reason, right? No one would just innocently and nonchalantly terminate rights to their children without a fight. I know I would fight Satan himself for my children. I would die for my children, for they are precious to me and a gift from God. I take pride in being a mother, for my greatest gift in life is the gift of motherhood. Unfortunately, it is a gift that so many women are not granted.

At age seventeen, I reconnected with one of my best friends from the Catholic high school I had attended while living with my adopted parents. Not long after, I went to live with her family, with the goal of finishing high school there. Her father was a teacher at the school. I was fortunate that they waived tuition for me since I was considered one of his children. While I was loved and accepted there, I continued to struggle with my ability to let my guard down and allow myself to be vulnerable.

I quickly found that, due to my lack of responsibility, I would have to repeat the eleventh grade since I was so far behind in my academics. This would prevent me from being able to graduate with the class of 1988. Therefore, I made the decision to drop out of high school instead of facing the predicament I allowed myself to be in. I felt like a failure, although my poor decisions to not complete homework assignments or study for tests had put me in that position. I had God-given ability and intelligence, but I did not apply it, and I was paying the price for my rebellion. I chose to run away from the situation instead of facing it. I left my friend's home and never returned. I did not even call them and tell them I was leaving. Instead, I just left. I did not care about anyone or anything, and it showed in my immature and poor decision that day. From there, I went to live with one of my uncles. I needed to figure out what my next step would be. It was also during this time that I located my biological brother through the adoption registry. He and one of my sisters had been adopted together. I still did not know where my youngest sister was, and it would be many years before we reconnected.

Shortly after turning eighteen years old, I decided to obtain my general educational development (GED) certificate instead of returning to a public school to finish high school. This led to getting my certified nurse aid (CNA) certification, with the goal of becoming a nurse one day. Looking back, I believe my search for the truth was guiding my decisions, whether they were good ones or bad ones. I was searching for my identity and purpose. It was a start to finding my way out of the mess I found myself in, one that I had caused all on my own. Even in the messes we create, God promises to help. "And we know that in all things God works for the good of those who love him, who have been called according to his purpose" (Romans 8:28). The point is that God can work through and turn *any* situation around, no matter how dire it looks. Although we may suffer the consequences of our actions, we should not lose hope, for He promises to sustain us, though we should stumble. There is always a lesson to be learned.

Then you will know the truth, and the truth will set you free.
—John 8:32

6

Receiving Grace

My grace is sufficient for you, for my power
is made perfect in weakness.

—2 Corinthians 12:9

GRACE IS GOD'S unmerited favor toward us. It is *love* in action toward people who do not deserve such love. It means that God pursues sinners to save us since we could not otherwise save ourselves. God demonstrated His love for us when He allowed His son, Jesus Christ, to be crucified on a cross to save humankind. He sent His son to free us from condemnation that we so rightfully deserved. "God made him who had no sin to be sin for us, so that in him we might become the righteousness of God" (2 Corinthians 5:21). God has led me to study the concept of grace in greater detail over the years. I never fully understood its meaning, since for so long I felt I had to *earn* God's favor or salvation somehow. Only through studying about grace did I learn that God could not love me any more than He already does, so no good work was going to earn His favor. I did not have to try to earn God's approval of me, nor did I have to be perfect in order to be loved. It was a given that God not only loved me but also approved of me. It did not mean there were not consequences to my actions. I still had to face the music regarding the poor choices I had made over the years. However, it was an assurance that I did not walk alone, that I could repent and be forgiven of my sins.

Lewis Sperry Chafer said, "So, also, grace finds its greatest triumph and glory in the sphere of human helplessness."[1] This demonstrates that God meets us where we are, even when we are at our ugliest and most helpless. He extends grace and shows compassion on a level that none of us deserve, but He still offers it freely. He longs to be gracious to us (see Isaiah 30:18). I do not believe any of us can live in total freedom without grasping fully what grace means.

At age eighteen, I started working at the local hospital as a CNA. I thoroughly enjoyed my new role and felt a sense of pride in caring for others. The nurses took me under their wings and taught me nursing skills. It strengthened my desire to pursue nursing as a career. I needed a way to pay for it, so in 1989, I joined the Oklahoma Army National Guard. I had taken a huge step out of my comfort zone. I made it through eight weeks of basic training, and it was tough. I tried to blend in with other recruits and do as I was told to not draw attention to myself. Midway through training, one of my drill sergeants called me to the front of the platoon and told me that I was the new squad leader for the fourth squad. I immediately began panicking inside. How could it be? I was not equipped or prepared to do that. What if the other recruits got upset with me? What if I failed? My mind thought of worst-case scenarios. However, I did not have a choice. I did as I was told, even if I did not want to, and I have to say that I did it very well. Perfectionism was always a driving force for me. I could not settle for anything less than being perfect. There was a cost to not doing things perfectly. Maybe I would be more lovable if I was. After bootcamp and advanced training as a combat medic, I returned home, where I decided to start prerequisites for nursing school. A few months later, I was called up for active duty, so I had to drop out of college to fulfill my military obligation. I was on active duty for about eight months before returning home. After returning, I decided to apply to licensed practical nursing (LPN) school, and I was accepted. It was a Monday-through-Friday obligation for a whole year. I worked nights at the local hospital as a CNA and attended school during the day. I was determined to make something out of my life, to get out of the awful situation I was in. I remember praying to God saying, "If You help me become a nurse, I will be the best nurse I can be." He answered my prayer, and for that I am most grateful. He put a strong desire in my heart to care for others, and I believe that one of my spiritual gifts is the gift of serving. Serving others became my passion. It was where I felt the happiest and the most rewarded.

When I was twenty-one years old, my biological mother suddenly passed away from a heart attack. She was only forty-two years old. She suffered with a severe panic disorder, and this apparently led to her death. I had just returned home after working the night shift at the hospital when I saw my father sitting on the couch, looking anxious. I could tell he had been crying. He told me that my mother had died during the night. I honestly felt no emotion—no sadness, nothing. At that time, I still had so much anger and resentment toward her that I did not really care. It would be many years before I grieved her death. Only once healing began in my heart could I break down the heart of stone I had developed over the years to allow God to soothe that painful area. Only then could I truly grieve my loss of not growing up with *my* mother, not the one the courts told me to call mom, not the one I never connected with, not the one who deeply loved me unconditionally and only wanted the best for me. I grieved the loss of the mother who had abandoned me, the one who never put me before her own needs, the one who abused me and allowed bad things to happen to me. I grieved for *my* birth mother, the one whose blood is running through my veins, the one who carried me for nine months and gave birth to me, the one I very much look like. This is who I longed to be loved and cherished by but, sadly, never fully was. I am happy to say that my mother had accepted Jesus as her Lord and Savior a few weeks before she died and is living in glory now. She is set free from the vines of hopelessness and despair that gripped her ever so tightly; free from addiction and anxiety; free from the emotional pain she suffered daily. This shows that God constantly pursues us, even to the very end.

My father died from a heart attack when I was twenty-four years old. He had just returned from work, and he told his sister that he needed to lie down before dinner. He apparently died peacefully in his sleep. This was comforting to me to know he did not suffer. I had not spoken with him in over a year, but nonetheless, I was heartbroken. A message had been left on our home answering machine from a family member, stating that my father had passed away. Fortunately, my husband listened to the message first while I was at the grocery store. He told me when I returned home, and I immediately felt numb, and then tears flowed. I cried out, "He wasn't saved! He wasn't saved!" In that moment, I begged and pleaded with God for my father to make it to heaven. You see, we all must choose to accept Jesus as our Lord and Savior in order to be rewarded with heaven. Jesus said, "I am the way and the truth and the life. No one comes to the Father except through me" (John 14:6). I strongly hold onto the belief that my continued prayers over the years for my father somehow allowed him to be given a second chance at salvation before dying, that in his last moment here on earth, he accepted Jesus Christ into his heart. While in prison, the apostle Paul and Silas said to the Philippian jailer, "Believe in the Lord Jesus, and you will be saved—you and your household" (Acts 16:31). This is a scripture I have held onto over the years when praying for family members who are not believers, having faith that one day, they too will be saved. I pray that I get to see my father again someday.

I have often pondered the thorn in the apostle Paul's side. Three times he asked God to remove it, only to be told, "My grace is sufficient for you, for my power is made perfect in weakness" (2 Corinthians 12:9). I often felt that if I was weak, I was a failure and inadequate, that I had to be perfect before I could approach the throne room of God. But when Jesus came to earth, He came full of grace. He brought with Him a way out of sin and a way back to God through true repentance.

I have struggled over the years in understanding how a loving, heavenly Father could allow His children to go through difficult and downright painful situations. To be honest, at times, it has caused me to question God's love for each and every one of us, as well as my ability to trust that He will guide and protect us. There must be a reason for all the pain, right? The apostle Paul went onto say, "Therefore I will boast all the more gladly about my weaknesses, so that Christ's power may rest on me. That is why, for Christ's sake, I delight in weaknesses, insults, in hardships, in persecutions, in difficulties. For when I am weak, then I am strong" (2 Corinthians 12:9–10). I believe Paul was telling us to stay faithful before the Lord and not to become self-centered and proud. It is easy to step out and try to do things in our own strength instead of relying on God and trusting that He knows best. However, God gave him grace to sustain him through all the hardships. He had God-given favor. It means I do not have to strive for perfectionism or feel like a failure when I am weak. I am learning that it is in my flaws and imperfections that grace shines through the brightest, giving God the glory. A perfect God still loves this imperfect girl anyway.

> Let us then approach God's throne of grace with
> confidence, so that we may receive mercy and
> find grace to help us in our time of need.
> —Hebrews 4:16

7

_____ ✑ _____

Virtuous Woman

A wife of noble character who can find?
She is worth far more than rubies.

—Proverbs 31:10

THROUGHOUT MY JOURNEY, God has been growing and
shaping me to become like a Proverbs 31 woman, one who is refined
and tested, for she is very precious to the Lord. She is strong and
capable and speaks with wisdom. Her husband and children arise
and call her blessed (see Proverbs 31). She makes the decision to get
up each day and put others' needs before her own. She can take what
seems ordinary and make it extraordinary. She is a world changer.
In her book _Secrets of the Proverbs 31 Woman_, Rae Simons stated,
"Doing those 'ordinary things' over and over and over sometimes
takes the most courage and strength of all-and those seemingly small

things are often what God uses to change the world."[1] This really spoke to me since I have so often measured my worth by my success. I strived to be the best in everything I attempted to do, and I often became hypercritical of myself and others for any shortcomings.

I am learning that *simple* is enough for me and that it is okay to not have it all together or figured out. I am very structured, and I like to have a plan, but sometimes that is not feasible, so I am learning to adapt to and overcome whatever comes my way. I am seeing that it is enough to get up every day, strive to be the best I can be, and not beat myself up when I fail. It is enough to love my family, be kind to my neighbors, and extend help to others. These are the qualities of a Proverbs 31 woman. This is all God is asking us to do. He is not asking for perfection. He is asking for a heart willing to love others. Jesus said in Mark 12:31, "Love your neighbor as yourself. There is no commandment greater than these." For life is precious, and my eyes are opening to see the beauty of it all, whether on the mountaintop or in the valley.

It was during LPN school in 1992 that I met my wonderful husband. God knew that I was a wounded girl, and I needed a man who was not afraid to show his emotions; one who was outgoing and strong but also gentle; one who would love me on my good days and even more on my bad days; one who would always support me and never abandon me, like so many people in my life had; one who would love me unconditionally and never hurt me. The man God chose for me exemplifies all of these qualities.

I was working at the local hospital when we met. He was a full-time fireman and also worked part-time for an ambulance service as an emergency medical technician (EMT). We had a mutual friend who introduced us. I knew I was going to marry him on our very first date, and that absolutely terrified me. I had never had a real relationship before, so it all was foreign to me. While I tried to turn off my feelings, something kept drawing me to him. There are many positive attributes that he manifests, but I have to say that his strength surpasses them all—not only his physical strength but his godly strength. I sensed something different in him, something I could not explain. Looking back, I have no doubt that God intervened and made sure our paths crossed.

My husband and I went on a date one evening. After dinner, he wanted to stop by and visit one of our friends who worked in the ER at the local hospital. She was the one who had introduced us. Well, to my surprise, that was where he proposed to me. He presented me with a long-stem red rose that had a ring dangling from it and a card saying, "Will you marry me?" I was both shocked and excited. I of course said yes. We dated for only six weeks before getting married. I am not an impulsive person, so this definitely was out of character for me, but I just knew in my heart I was to marry this man. We were married at the county courthouse by a judge on June 26, 1992. It was a simple wedding; just the two witnesses were present. There was a small reception that followed, with only a few people attending. It was one of the happiest days of my life. It felt good to be loved and valued.

In the beginning, married life seemed foreign. I did not know the first thing about how to function in a stable, loving relationship, but I dove in with both feet and quickly learned to tread water. My husband and I are opposites, so we had to learn to accept each other's differences and not see them as limitations. Over the years, he has made comments about how he does not understand why I feel and act the way I do, but it is something that I cannot explain or even understand myself. He is very much an extrovert. There are times when I have asked God to take away my shyness and to make me a little bolder and more outgoing, but I am now learning to accept me for me and to not be ashamed of who I am. I am learning to be happy with who God created, shyness and all. How boring life would be if we were all the same. Where we see flaws, God sees colors and beauty.

I have no doubt that being married to someone with such a troubled past has been difficult for my husband, but he has stuck by me and never wavered in his love and commitment to me. God has given him barrels of grace to sustain him over the years. I believe my lack of self-worth played a pivotal role in how I viewed and understood relationships. I was a broken girl trying to put the pieces back together, but I had no idea how to do it. At that time in my life, I was very much a baby Christian, and I was only really beginning my walk with Jesus. I still needed to fully grasp the importance of allowing Him to be my beacon of light through the darkness. For that was the only way I would have the courage to face the darkness and allow healing to come forth. Amazingly, God put me in the Thomas family, where, in time, I would feel safe enough to confront the unknown. Trust was being built. Jesus said, "I am the light of the world. Whoever follows me will never walk in darkness, but will have the light of life" (John 8:12).

A father is supposed to be the first man a little girl loves. Men are supposed to be the leaders, protectors, and providers of their families. Research confirms how important a father is in the development of a child's self-esteem, their relationships, establishing positive coping skills, and overall life choices. I fully believe that God created the father-daughter bond to set the foundation for her relationship with her future husband.

When researching the importance of this type of a relationship, I saw firsthand how the lack of it could be detrimental to a child's normal development. Well-known Christian psychologist Dr. James Dobson stated, "Fathers have an incalculable impact on their daughters."[2] I have no doubt this is the case since if a little girl is told by her father that she is beautiful and worthy, she will believe it. She will seek out a man in the future who values her and sees her worth, since this was engrained in her from an early age. Dobson further stated, "That all future romantic relationships to occur in a girl's life will be influenced positively or negatively by the way she perceives and interacts with her dad."[3] Unfortunately, this foundation was not established as a little girl in my life, so I feel it limited me early on in my marriage. However, God promises to never leave us without help. He sent the Holy Spirit to guide us through our journey if we allow Him to, and He has been instrumental in my marriage. I am happy to say that my husband and I will celebrate twenty-eight years of marriage this year, and we are still going strong!

Our first son was born in 1993. I still remember taking this precious baby boy home and wondering how I would care for him since I knew absolutely nothing about taking care of a baby. There was no one there to show me. On most days, it was just God and me. Of course, my husband helped when he could, but he worked twenty-four-hour shifts at the fire department, as well as the ambulance service, so he was not home very much. All I knew was that I deeply loved my baby, and this seemed such a foreign emotion to me, one that I had never experienced before. It was just engrained in me to love this little person so deeply. I loved with a momma's heart. This is the way God designed us to love—unconditional, vast love.

Well, I fell into the role of motherhood and learned how to nurture and care for my son. Looking back over the years, I have no doubt that the Holy Spirit guided me through, teaching and showing me how to care for my children in such a loving and responsible way. I most certainly did not want to follow in the footsteps of my birth mother, so a new path had to be paved. The unhealthy cycle had to be broken.

Two years and ten months later, my youngest son was born. During my pregnancy with him, I often questioned how I was going to love this little one as much as I loved his older brother. I feared that I would not know how. I quickly learned that there was enough love for both of them, for my heart just expanded to a size that had enough love. This is so amazing to me. I am in awe of how the heavenly Father works. The parental bond and foundation of trust was established in my sons' lives at birth. They were safe, nurtured, and loved deeply by both their mother and father. It was extremely important to me that they not have the same childhood I had, so I went above and beyond to make sure they did not, sometimes even to the extreme.

I had the strong urge to constantly pray over my children and even begged God to keep anything bad from happening to them. I was terrified of them being taken away from me somehow. I was overprotective in those early years. It was not until I learned to trust God, really trust Him, that I began to loosen the reigns of control. I was a momma bear protecting her babies. No one was going to hurt or mistreat my children—no one!

I lacked the understanding that it is only through trials and the battles of life that we become stronger and able to endure valiantly. Hebrews 11:34 outlines this very thing. "Whose weakness was turned to strength; and who became powerful in battle." As a child learns to walk, this is much like our faith. Although a child may stumble in the beginning and even fall, if they continue trying and do not give up, they will eventually learn to walk. Faith is much like this; it is like a muscle and must be exercised and stretched in order to grow, no matter how painful it is.

For it is in the crushing, in the pressing that growth and newness occurs. Jesus said the following:

> No one sews a patch of unshrunk cloth on an old garment, for the patch will pull away from the

garment, making the tear worse. Neither do people pour new wine into old wineskins. If they do, the skins will burst; the wine will run out and the wineskins will be ruined. No, they pour new wine into new wineskins, and both are preserved. (Matthew 9:16–17)

The strength of fermentation of the new wine would be too much for the partly worn out, filthy vessels. The holes that would form would allow an entry for the enemy to get a foothold in. He is ruthless. So, if we never changed or grew, it would be impossible for the Holy Spirit to dwell in us. We have to throw off the old me and put on the new me. "Therefore, if anyone is in Christ, the new creation has come: The old has gone, the new is here!" (2 Corinthians 5:17).

One of my favorite stories is an inspirational story about a beautiful little teacup. The teacup did not start out as beautiful. Instead, it was a lump of clay that had to be molded and shaped into its beauty, often with much stress and tension. The process was painful and seemed to be unending. However, the potter knew just how much to push to prevent the teacup from cracking under pressure. During the molding, the teacup did not understand why it had to endure such pain and struggle. It felt like giving up and continued to cry out to the potter, asking, "How much longer?" more or less saying, "Where are you, God?" In the end, the teacup was given a mirror to see firsthand the change that had occurred through the process. The teacup did not recognize itself and said, "That's not me; that couldn't be me. It's beautiful. I'm beautiful." It saw the beauty it became through the molding and shaping. The story teaches us to endure to the end and not fall into the temptation of giving up but, instead, to press through the pain and struggle. For if we do, we will reap the beautifulness and uniqueness of the end journey. But, oh how many times I have wanted to throw in the towel and just give up! To just turn and run away from all the sorrow and adversities of life. But much like the little teacup, I am now allowing my maker to change me, so I can become the best version of *me*.

Interestingly, the teacup never cursed the potter. Instead, it continued to cry out to Him. The potter never once became angry with the teacup for asking questions or even for doubting Him. Instead, the potter showed much compassion in answering the teacup by saying, "Not yet," as if He understood and almost expected the questions.[4] This shows that the heavenly Father truly understands our struggles, doubts, and lack of faith at times. He wants to mold, shape, and form us from a lump of hard clay into His beautiful masterpiece, if we only let Him. "Like clay in the hand of the potter, so are you in my hand" (Jeremiah 18:6).

Mark 9:21–24 tells the story of a boy who was stricken with convulsions. The boy's father had taken him to where Jesus was ministering to others, believing that Jesus could heal his son. Jesus asked the man how long his child had been ill, and the father answered, "From childhood." He further stated, "But if you can do anything, take pity on us and help us." Jesus responded, "If you can? Everything is possible for one who believes." The man responded, "I do believe; help me overcome my unbelief!" To be honest, I have often cried out similarly on my own behalf, asking Jesus to help me overcome my unbelief. This often follows times when I want circumstances to move a little faster than what I see happening, more or less trying to force them in my own time, or when I do not see the answer I am seeking come forth. Instead, God is stretching and teaching me through the circumstances, telling me that He knows what is best for me. He is saying, "Not yet. Trust me." I am learning to drown out the voice of the enemy and instead listen to the voice of the Lord encouraging me to stay the course and not waver in my belief.

I have grown leaps and bounds through my journey of marriage and motherhood. While some days are rougher than others, I am grateful for each day, no matter what it brings. I have a blueprint to guide me along the way to becoming a virtuous woman, one who is brave, walks in integrity, helps the needy, loves her husband, and teaches her children to serve God. But above all, she fears the Lord.[5] I strive to emulate these qualities in my life daily.

Charm is deceptive, and beauty is fleeting; but a woman who fears the Lord is to be praised.

—Proverbs 31:30

8

Pursuing Strength

So do not fear, for I am with you; do not be dismayed,
for I am your God. I will strengthen you and help you;
I will uphold you with my righteous right hand.

—Isaiah 41:10

JESUS SAID THAT in this life we would have trouble, but if we cling to Him, we will make it through. Our job is to remain steadfast during times of adversity, for we are always promised a way out. Through it, we will not be shaken if He is holding our hand (see Psalm 16:8). Learning to hold His hand and face the darkness was difficult for me, since I preferred to turn and run away from it. However, eventually I was pushed out of my safety net and forced to face the darkness head-on.

My healing journey went into full force in my late twenties. Apparently, God felt it was time for all those buried emotions to finally surface, and it felt like a floodgate was opened. It would have been much easier if healing had come instantaneously instead of having to walk it through. However, God is in control, and I am not, which was something I still had to learn.

When I was twenty-seven years old, I was struggling more and more with depression, so my sister-in-law recommended I try an over-the-counter herbal medication that was supposed to help with it. Instead, it caused severe anxiety that led to panic attacks. I found myself going from not feeling much emotion over anything to suddenly feeling everything. I was spiraling out of control and could not stop it. The anxiety was so intense that I could not even watch TV without having a panic attack. I was not sleeping or eating, and I had difficulty focusing on the simplest of tasks. Anxiety consumed me, and it was awful.

I even got to the point where I contemplated suicide on more than one occasion, just to stop the pain I was feeling. I only wanted to feel numb and hide inside my cocoon once again. I prayed nonstop, begging God to take the anxiety away. Thinking about my children and how devastated they would feel if I took my life was the *only* thing that stopped me. I would look at their pictures and cry, thinking about being separated from them, but I just wanted the pain to stop.

I stood in my living room shouting out loud Psalm 91, holding onto every word, hoping that somehow hearing it would dull the anxiety. I reached out to one of my best friends and Christian mentor to ask for prayer. She encouraged me to stand on God's Word and to not waver, no matter how I felt, but I just did not know how to accomplish this. I was still very much a baby Christian, and I felt

COURAGE THROUGH THE DARKNESS

inept most days. But Jesus said we only need the faith of a mustard seed to move mountains. "Because you have so little faith. Truly I tell you, if you have faith as small as a mustard seed, you can say to this mountain, 'Move from here to there,' and it will move. Nothing will be impossible for you" (Matthew 17:20). I clung to this scripture, believing that eventually I would be okay, even if I did not see progress in that moment. It was a spark of faith that still needed to be ignited.

I continued to work as a nurse during this time, but it was getting more difficult with each passing day, especially since I was not sleeping well. My mind was a mess, limiting my ability to concentrate. I believe that when our minds are full of anxiety and cannot slow down to rest, this is when the enemy attacks the hardest. It is when we lack the ability to guard our minds effectively, leaving an open door for the enemy to gain entry.

While trying to doze on my lunchbreak at work one day, I heard, "Be anxious for nothing," and I had a strong urge to go to a local Christian bookstore. While browsing through the books, I saw one by author and well-known Christian speaker, Joyce Meyer, named, "Be Anxious for Nothing: The Art of Casting Your Cares and Resting in God."[1] I just about fell over when I saw it. I quickly purchased the book and started reading it immediately, devouring every word in order to try to find some peace to the turmoil of emotions I felt. At that point, I saw emotions as the enemy, and I tried everything to shove them back into a box instead of learning to accept and grow with them.

From there, I read several more books by Joyce Meyer on how to effectively manage emotions, as well as how to win the raging battle in the mind. I was slowly learning that I did not have to let my emotions manage me. Instead, emotions are God given and normal.

I just needed to learn how to manage them more effectively. I had always kept my emotions in check and only allowed myself to feel certain things, like loving my children, since it was much safer to not feel. I even kept my husband at a distance and had never fully showed him love on the level that God designed for a husband and wife to share.

It was during this time that I started seeing a psychologist to help me gain some perspective into what I was feeling. He encouraged me to start journaling my thoughts. I started writing, but the words did not flow easily, so instead, I began writing to the Lord, telling Him how much I loved and appreciated Him. God put in my heart one day to thank Him that I was the apple of His eye. This seemed so foreign to me since I did not feel like the apple of anyone's eye, so it was very difficult to do. The words did not come easily out of my mouth. They almost felt forced. However, the more I said them, the easier it became and the more I believed them.

I told the psychologist that I would able to handle my emotions *only* if God promised nothing bad would ever happen to me or my loved ones again. He told me that this was not possible, for we live in a fallen world. I became angry that I could not control the situation. My whole life, I had tried to stay one step ahead of disaster, so I was constantly striving to control everything around me. I tried to never allow myself to be in any situation where I could not see a way out, and I most certainly did not allow others into the very small *circle* I had placed around myself. I was very much guarded. Early on, the only way I could control my response to any given situation was to bury my emotions and place a lock on the box. So now, I was being told to not only allow my emotions to surface but to *feel* them while continuing to face whatever life threw at me. I was on unsteady ground and no longer able to hide anymore. I felt terrified and out of control.

Jesus clearly told us that we will face tribulations in this fallen world. He never promised us a bed of roses but that He would be there with us every step of the way when we faced adversity. "I have told you these things, so that in me you may have peace. In this world you will have trouble. But take heart! I have overcome the world" (John 16:33). Clearly, we are to cling to Jesus and not lose hope when facing difficulties. This was something I struggled to do, but I made the choice to keep moving forward no matter how I felt.

I enjoyed my sessions with the psychologist, and I continued to slowly accept that my emotions were not the enemy. I was also learning positive coping skills to help steer me in life. One particular session, grief took over, and I sat on the floor, much like a child, and laid my head against the psychologist's leg. Initially, this appeared to take him off guard, but then he just gently patted me on the head, telling me I was okay as I sat there sobbing. I rarely cried for myself, so this was something new and a huge step, to say the least. He consoled me that day much like a parent consoles a hurting child. Layer by layer, the grief was being released, and I was learning to accept my God-given emotions, no matter how scared I felt.

Showing emotions did not come easily for me, unlike my husband. He is 6'5" and towers over most people. He is outgoing and social. His heart matches his larger-than-life personality. Things just seem to come easily for him. In contrast, I struggle with social skills and prefer to stay to myself. I have a small circle of friends, and I prefer it that way. Trust is earned in my books, so I have to feel close to a person before I can share anything personal. So, believe me, sharing my story with the world is a *huge* leap of faith and is taking me completely out of my comfort zone.

One of my biggest fears early on in our marriage was meeting new people. When socializing, I often found myself standing behind my husband, trying to make myself invisible. I would hyperventilate when thinking about having to converse with others. He has told me over the years that I just need to just start talking and engaging in conversation. This is a much easier task for an extrovert. I am learning day by day to step out in faith and do it anyway. Amazingly, it gets easier the more I do it. Fear loses its hold as we face it, for we become stronger.

In 1999, my older sister, her husband, my two sons, and I went to the local recreation center to swim. My brother-in-law sat by the kiddie pool to watch my sons, ages five and three, swim. There were large floating devices in the pool, which apparently limited the lifeguard's view of the kiddie pool. I was unaware of this at the time. My sister and I decided to play racquetball, so we made our way toward the door. She suddenly turned around and looked back in the direction of the kiddie pool. In that moment, I saw my youngest son submerge underwater, and no one else saw him do it—not my brother-in-law, who was reading, and not the lifeguard, who was focused on the larger pool. My sister screamed, "He is drowning!" and we both ran toward the pool. My brother-in-law reached the pool first and pulled my son from the water. My son immediately began coughing and crying. The lifeguard cried too. She was only seventeen years old, with a great deal of responsibility put on her. I comforted my son for a short while before introducing him back into the water. Although he was fearful and kept a close hold on me, he sat with me in the pool. I knew that if I did not expose him to the water right away, he could develop a fear of swimming or water in general. For several months after the incident, he cried during his baths. I continued to soothe and comfort him, telling him it was okay and that he was safe. When we returned home after leaving the recreation center that day, I woke my husband up to inform him of the incident. He was working nights at the time. After telling him, he asked what time this happened. I told him around 3:00 pm. He started crying. He said that he went back to bed around 3:00 p.m., since he had gotten up to watch NFL football. When he got back into bed, he heard, "Ryan drowning" in his spirit and immediately started praying for his son. I have no doubt our son is alive today due to my husband's obedience to pray at that moment! Praise God for His protection over my son that day! This is why praying and pleading the blood of Jesus over your family members is so important. For it puts a hedge of protection around them that the enemy cannot penetrate. Once I learned to do this, it was like a lightbulb came on in me. For so long, I tried to control everything around me, even though I could not. However, God gave us a weapon in the spiritual realm to use, one that the enemy has no control over. This is how we are to fight our battles. This is something my husband and I pray over our family members daily.

In 2007, my oldest son and I were in a kitchen fire, requiring both of us to need skin graft surgery. I was working in the intensive care unit at the time and had worked several night shifts in a row. I was not adjusting well to the night shift, which limited my ability to sleep more than a few hours during the day. Out of sleep deprivation, I made a decision that could have cost my son his life. When I woke up in the afternoon, I suddenly felt an urge to put my cotton socks on but quickly talked myself out of it. Later, I found out how this decision would play into the situation.

My son had put cooking oil in a pot on the stove to make french fries. He got busy watching TV and soon forgot about the pot. When he remembered, he ran to the kitchen, where I saw him remove the lid from the pot of very hot grease. A small flame shot out of it. In my sleep-deprived moment, I panicked and told him to put water on it. He did as I told him to do. He walked the pot over to the sink and proceeded to put it under the water faucet, causing a ten-foot flash fire. It literally blew up in his face. I saw him turn his head to the side, trying to pull back from flames while they climbed up to the ceiling, over his head, into the dining room and living room. I panicked and yelled, "Throw the pan!" and he did, directly onto my sockless legs. We both slipped on the grease on the floor and fell down. Immediately I jumped up, ran to the garage, and was able to get the fire out with a fire extinguisher. I noticed the skin blistering on my lower legs and left foot. Once the adrenalin wore off, I felt an intense burning pain where I had been burned. My son had a burn on his right forearm that was also starting to blister.

A thought popped into my head, *Break the lipid bilayer.* I knew what this meant from microbiology many years before. However, I do not talk this way. Looking back, I knew it had to be the Holy Spirit directing my steps. My son and I went into the bathroom and sat fully clothed in the bathtub with cool water pouring over our burns. You see, if I had been wearing my cotton socks, I possibly would not have sustained as deep of burns as I did. I aggressively started rubbing the burns with a washcloth to break the lipid layer and allow the cool water to penetrate. Only the Holy Spirit could have guided me to do this!

My husband was at work, so I called him and told him what happened. He sent one of his fellow police officers to check on us while he was on his way home. I then called my father-in-law and said, "Let me tell you what God did for my son," as I was hysterically crying. While I was in shock over the accident, I was also in complete and total awe at seeing the hand of God move on my son's behalf; only God could have protected him from those flames! Amazingly, he did not have one burn on his face, nor was his airway affected in any way. I have no doubt that angels surrounded him that day, shielding and protecting him. Psalm 91 was in full effect. He had the Blood of Jesus covering him. That flame was right there in his face. I am so thankful my son is alive and here today in spite of the poor decision I made. To God be all the glory!

I learned a powerful lesson that day. Here I thought I was the one protecting my children, trying to do things in my own might and strength, but it was actually God who protects us all, for He is sovereign. A stupid, sleep-deprived decision on my part could have cost my son his very life. This situation opened my eyes, and it became a stepping-stone in my journey to really learning to trust God on a greater level than I ever had before. It showed me that He is the captain of the ship, and I am not. I needed to stop looking at the size of the storm and instead look to the one who controls the storms and seas. How freeing this was for me. "But the fear of God reigning in the heart is the beauty of the soul; it lasts forever" (Matthew Henry, 2).

One of my favorite pictures is of a little girl sitting in a swing, swinging back and forth, with her hair blowing in the wind. She has the biggest smile on her face and looks so content and carefree. She is enjoying herself immensely, without a worry in the world. However, instead of the ropes on the swing being attached to a metal bar, her Creator is holding them between His thumb and index finger. But this did not sway the joy she displayed, for this little girl trusted that He would never let go. I have often looked at this picture and pondered what it would be like to trust with such innocence and intention. It is the childlike faith that is required of us all. The way I saw God protect my son the day he was burned caused my faith to grow. Although God did not stop the incident from happening, He protected us *through* it since it could have been so much worse. This parallels with my childhood. While God did not stop the storms I faced, He got me *through* it.

Leslie Gould said, "Sometimes God calms the storm, but sometimes God lets the storm rage and calms His Child."[3] He chose that day to calm us through the storm instead of stopping it, for it allowed me to see that not every end result is always bad, that I need to search for any positive that comes out of it. It caused me to look with a glass-half-full view instead of glass-half-empty. I saw how mighty God was in that moment and that I was the one limiting Him. For so many years, I put Him in a box, limiting His sovereignty in my life. This is exactly what Sharon P. cautioned me to never do. I looked at situations using adult faith instead of childlike faith. Walking through this adversity without falling apart or trying to control the outcome was a definite step toward learning to walk in a childlike faith that I so desperately needed.

When I turned forty years old, I had a dream of me holding a baby girl. In it, I was speaking to my husband and said, "Look, honey, we have the baby girl we always wanted," and I woke up. I knew it meant something spiritual. I believe this was setting the stage for the final step in my long journey of healing. He was telling me that it was time to be completely healed, for He had set all the pieces in motion. He had brought this wounded girl into this wonderful family and engulfed her with love like she had never felt before, to let her know that she was safe, protected, and surrounded by people who cherished her. Now it was time to release *all* of the trauma.

Several months later, I saw the manifestation of this dream. While standing in my room one night, I was anxious over a situation, and I felt angry at myself for feeling that way and not trusting God. It was like my heart wanted so desperately to trust God, but my mind would not allow it. It is easy to say we trust Him but entirely different to actually walk it out with unwavering faith. You see, over the years, I would *give it to God*; then, out of fear, I would take it back and try to fix the situation in my own strength. It was exhausting.

I stood there crying out to the Lord, begging Him to heal me once and for all and to take *all* of my fears away. I felt desperate and broken. Through my grief and tears, I began screaming at the devil in anger, commanding him to leave me alone. I said, "I draw a line in the sand, and fear does not control me anymore, in Jesus's name." With my right foot, I drew an actual line across the carpet in a way, validating my decision. This time I meant it. I immediately felt a change. A boldness like I had never felt before suddenly came over me. In that instant, I moved from fear to faith. I stepped out from the familiar into the unknown, trusting that God would be there to get me through.

I called my father-in-law and told him what had happened. He said, "God wants me to tell you that He has been waiting on this, waiting for you to take a stand." God wants us to take a stand, to draw a line and tell the enemy he has no right to cross it, to trust God's every word. It had taken me years to get to that point, but once there, I found it so incredibly simple. Even if I did not know it, I was on God's radar. He was watching, protecting, and guiding my every footstep through the dark, gloomy early years of my life, knowing that one day He would raise me up and set me free from the bondage of my past.

Several weeks after this incident, God gave me a dream of this very thing, telling me, "For I have placed your feet on a new foundation for which they will never come down off of. It is finished." In my dream, I saw myself being lifted into the air feetfirst and being placed on a tall white pillar. From that point on, I have felt different, more alive and free than ever before. It is also when many of my childhood fears lost their grip on me. It was the beginning of childlike faith developing in my heart. It made sense of the dream God had given me about the baby girl that had been born. In a way, it was a new birth. My journey had brought me to this point, teaching me that although my life was not always easy, with many bumps and bruises along the way, it forced me to become a strong and capable woman of God through adversity. This is something I will always cherish, since I felt safe for the first time in a very long time.

> The name of the Lord is a strong tower; the
> righteous run to it and are safe.
> —Proverbs 18:10 NKJV

9

⸎

Learning to Forgive

Get rid of all bitterness, rage and anger, brawling and slander,
along with every form of malice. Be kind and compassionate to one
another, forgiving each other, just as in Christ God forgave you.
—Ephesians 4:31–32

THE BIBLE TELLS us to forgive those who hurt us, although
I have found this to be easier said than done. However, if we truly
want to receive God's best, as well as His forgiveness for our own sins,
then we must forgive. It is conditional on our part. There are many
people bound up with unforgiveness who continue to give control
to the very one(s) who hurt them. We do not forgive solely for the
offender. Instead, we forgive so we can be set free from vines that can
choke the very life from us. In Matthew 6:14–15, Jesus said, "For if
you forgive other people when they sin against you, your heavenly

67

Father will also forgive you. But if you do not forgive others their sins, your Father will not forgive your sins." It takes *courage* to forgive those who have hurt you so deeply. However, Jesus plainly tells us that we will not be forgiven if we do not forgive.

I recently visited with one of my biological uncles, my mother's oldest brother, who I had not spoken to in almost ten years. He told me that he and his wife had cared for my siblings and me off and on since our birth. One particular time, he said we had been living with him for about six months before my mother called, asking for us to be returned to her. He was reluctant, fearing that we would just go back into the same unhealthy environment we came out of. So he spoke with my grandmother to seek her advice about what he should do. She told him that she was hopeful my mother would change this time, so he optimistically returned us to her care. He said not even two weeks later, we were taken once again by DHS and placed back into the foster care system for one final time before adoption. He drove to the county courthouse, pleading for the court to allow him to become our guardian, but the judge denied the request. He said he was devastated over this decision. I heard the anguish in his voice as he told me this story. I cannot tell you how much this touched my heart—to hear that I actually was wanted and fought for by someone in my family.

However, after much thought, I was glad the judge denied the request, since it would have changed the direction my path took me in life. Although painful, I honestly would not change one thing in my life since it has made me who I am today. My past has allowed me to develop a compassion and empathy for others that I am not sure I would have developed without facing the struggles and challenges I battled and overcame. It was in those difficulties that God revealed Himself to me the greatest and where I often have felt the closest to Him. He taught me to forgive those who hurt me. In my younger years as a baby Christian, forgiveness was very difficult for me. I did not understand why we are instructed to forgive others since I felt I was letting the offender off the hook. When I really read the Bible and studied what it said about forgiveness, I learned that it actually would help *me* to heal. In addition to forgiving others, I had to also learn to forgive myself. The latter was the hardest of all. I had to let myself off the hook and love myself in order to ever fully love anyone else. You see, in some strange way, I blamed myself for the abuse that I endured.

Shame and guilt were strong emotions that I felt daily for so long. I was ashamed about the way I looked, acted, and felt. I just wanted to hide from the world. I felt like a failure in life, and I did not know how to recover. I thought if I could just limit my surroundings, I would somehow feel better. The filth that covered me felt too heavy to bear, so I further alienated myself, hoping it would help in some way, but it never did. The deep wounds of childhood trauma continued to surface, and there was no stopping them. Only once I drew closer to Jesus did I see the answer through scripture. It was where I saw how to conquer and defeat the Goliath of shame and guilt in my life once and for all.

The first step was realizing that I was an innocent victim in the abuse I suffered and that I did not have to let it continue victimizing me into adulthood. I could choose to become a victor instead of a victim. I had to release my shame to the Lord and *forgive* not only my abusers but also myself. I learned that the shame I felt belonged to the abuser(s) alone; it was not mine to carry.

Many years ago, I came across a scripture that I have since held on to. I often read this scripture just to remind me of the promise God put down in my heart. "But all who devour you will be devoured; all your enemies will go into exile. Those who plunder you will be plundered; all who make spoil of you I will despoil. But I will restore you to health and heal your wounds', declares the Lord, 'because you are called an outcast, Zion for whom no one cares'" (Jeremiah 30:16-17). The first time I read this, I felt like someone actually cared for me, even to the point of going to battle for me. For as long as I could remember, I battled for myself. Always in fight mode, I was ready to defend my very existence. It softened me to the point where I was able to put my guard down, just a little. I had a promise from the Lord that He had my back and I would never be alone since He loved me.

But first, I had to understand what *love* even meant. I often pondered why God created humans in the first place. Looking around, I saw so much pain and sorrow, so I could not fathom our very existence. How could He still love us although we are sinners? How can He stand to see all the troubles in the world? A quote that resonates with me says, "Forgiveness is the best form of love. It takes a strong person to say sorry and an even stronger person to forgive."[1] For, "Love is patient, love is kind. It does not envy, it does not boast, it is not proud. It does not dishonor others, it is not self-seeking, it is not easily angered, it keeps no record of wrongs. Love does not delight in evil but rejoices with the truth. It always protects, always trusts, always hopes, always perseveres" (1 Corinthians 13:4–7).

But what does this mean? In the simplest of terms, it means God is love, for love is made complete only through Him. (See 1 John 16.) Furthermore, "There is no fear in love. But perfect love drives out fear, because fear has to do with punishment. The one who fears is not made perfect in love" (1 John 4:18). Love is the root and foundation of all good relationships. It is a gift from our heavenly Father, but it requires action on our part. For if we truly love God, then we will want to extend His love to others. He demonstrated His love for us by allowing Jesus to die on the cross for our sins. This selfless act demonstrates agape love at its finest. The apostle Paul encourages us to "be imitators of God ... and walk in love, as Christ also has loved us and given Himself for us, an offering and a sacrifice to God…" (see Ephesians 5:1–2 NKJV).

Therefore, I strive to show this type of love to others, a love that is selfless and unconditional even if not reciprocated. It is not keeping score when I feel I have been wronged. It is being quick to forgive those who I feel have wronged me and not holding grudges against them. It is just loving people no matter what. It was like the lightbulb came on when I finally understood the meaning of love from our Creator's viewpoint. For *this* is why we were created … to love as He loves.

Part of being healed from one's past is being able to look beyond the emotion and forgive others, no matter what pain they may have caused you. This is the true act of forgiveness. This is eventually what happened with my mother; I forgave her. It was not easy, but I did it. I saw how her own struggles caused her to withdrawal to the point where she could not be the person God called her to be. She was full of bitterness and unforgiveness that poisoned her soul and caused her to spiral out of control. The cycle needed to be broken, but she did not know how, so it continued. This is how the enemy works. He causes torment in the mind, and unless the Word of God is deeply rooted in a person, the foundation crumbles. I have only been able to understand this as I have matured and faced my own dysfunction. It was so much easier to forgive my father than my mother, but eventually I got there. By forgiving my parents for their shortcomings, I extended grace to them, as I have been shown grace for my own shortcomings. Only by grace could I forgive them.

In addition, I forgave my molesters and anyone else I felt led to forgive. I spoke the person's name out loud and said, "I forgive you for" and named the offense. I then boldly told each one that they do not have control over me anymore, that they lost their power and can no longer hurt me, in Jesus's name. Lastly, I released them and the offense(s) to the Lord, putting it in His hands now, finally freeing myself of the weight.

It was challenging in the beginning to forgive them since the enemy was constantly in my ear, telling me otherwise, for the pain was still so raw even after so many years. However, the Holy Spirit gently reminded me that by forgiving them, I was not validating what they did to me; instead, it was releasing them to God and allowing the scab to fully heal into a scar. While I will always remember the injustice I faced, it is now just a part of my journey and no longer has me stuck, limiting my ability to move forward in life.

You see, if I was not able to forgive those who had hurt me, then how could our heavenly Father forgive me of my sins? I knew that I had a choice—to hold onto my anger and bitterness, letting it consume me in a deep, dark hole of despair, or I could *choose* to give it to God and allow Him to heal my brokenness and restore me. The choice was ultimately mine. God was not going to force me. He was persistent in encouraging me to forgive so I could receive the healing and blessings He desired for me. "Forgiveness does not change the past, but it does change the future."[1] God had given me the grace to forgive. Now I had to make the decision to accept it, move forward, and leave my past to Him (see Philippians 3:13–14).

I have found that it is in our brokenness that God's light shines the brightest through the cracked and painful areas of our heart. He promises to restore us and give us beauty for ashes. However, we must choose to lay our ashes down at the foot of the cross or we will never receive the beauty He desires to give us. Forgiveness was the key to being set free, and grace gave me the power to lay my ashes down.

To bestow on them a crown of beauty instead of ashes, the oil
of joy instead of mourning, and a garment of praise instead of
a spirit of despair. They will be called oaks of righteousness,
a planting of the Lord for the display of his splendor.

—Isaiah 61:3

10

———— ❧ ————

Finding Freedom

So if the Son sets you free, you will be free indeed.
—John 8:36

MY LIFE NOW envelops freedom, for I know who I am in Christ. This type of freedom could only come through complete surrender to the Lord Jesus Christ. Surrender means fully giving up one's own will to the will of the Father, relinquishing yourself to God with the goal of pursuing Him fully. It is stepping out in faith and trusting unconditionally. My surrender came when I got fed up with the direction my life was going. The burden was too great to continue carrying on my own. I had to make the choice to surrender it to the Lord, no matter how ugly or familiar it was.

By doing this, it allowed the heavy load that I carried for so many years to fall off and complete freedom to come forth. Fear lost its grip on me, shame and guilt disappeared, and being an overcomer prevailed. This is the freedom that God wanted me to have all along. I was released from the chains of my past, from failures and the shackles of oppression. The only way to obtain this and to be truly set free was to fully know that I am a child of God. It meant throwing off the misconception and lies that had been engrained deep in my soul. It meant I had to renew how I thought in order to win the raging battle in my mind.

The apostle Paul said, "It is for freedom that Christ has set us free. Stand firm, then, and do not let yourselves be burdened again by a yoke of slavery" (Galatians 5:1). To me, this means we now live under God's grace, which is freely given. Paul also said, "For sin shall no longer be your master, because you are not under law, but under grace" (Romans 6:14). However, this does not give us a pass to continue sinning. Instead, it shows that when we do sin, we can repent and move forward, trying to be a better version of ourselves, one that is pleasing to God.

Furthermore, Paul talked about nine characteristics each believer should manifest in their lives. The fruits of the spirit are love, joy, peace, patience, kindness, goodness, faithfulness, gentleness, and self-control (see Galatians 5:22–23). These characteristics take time to grow and develop in our lives, much like fruit has to be ripened. The Holy Spirit helps us grow in these characteristics as we reject our old sinful ways. The more we grow in the ways of the Lord, sinful desires no longer appeal to us as they once did. Thus, our spirit grows stronger.

One of my favorite scriptures that I read quite often is, "Do not conform to the pattern of this world, but be transformed by the renewing of your mind. Then you will be able to test and approve what God's will is-his good, pleasing and perfect will" (Romans 12:2).

My mind is where Satan torments me the most, for it is where the harshest of memories and feelings manifested and where fear took its initial hold. If one has not struggled in this area, it can be difficult to understand why a person acts or responds the way they do. Trauma can rewire the brain, making it difficult for positive growth and healthy relationships to develop. One of the things I have anguished over is not having one person in my life who has been present from birth to now. I have had many relationships with people coming in and out of my life but never a constant one. This is why it was so difficult for me to establish strong bonds with others. I knew the cycle had to be broken for the sake of future generations. I vowed to give my children the stability I did not have. As I have grown my relationship with Jesus, I now see that He was there all along. He is and will always be the constant in my life. He was there in that little house on Littel Street holding my hand when I wept, as well as any other painful times in my life; I just did not know it at the time. To help me through, He gave me a strong will to never give up.

My strong will has served me well over the years. It gave me the drive to not settle and to keep striving, to find a different door if one is closed, in order to pursue the right one. In 2004, I had doors shut when I returned to college to pursue my registered nursing degree. I had been an LPN for fourteen years and felt it was time to advance my career. I worked full-time and had two little boys at home and a husband. I was busy enough already, but I felt a peace and strong desire in my heart to step out in faith. However, it was not an easy task. Due to not graduating high school and only having a GED, I was required to take several placement tests. I took them at the local university where I wanted to attend nursing school. I passed all but one. I miserably failed the science placement test, and I am a science major. I was told that I needed to take a basic remedial science course in order to enroll in cellular biology. I was devastated.

I thought about just throwing in the towel, but my stubbornness and type A personality would not let me. I knew if they just would let me in the class, I would do well, but the answer was no. If I decided to take the remedial course, it would set me back a whole year in being able to apply to the nursing program. So, I tried a different door. I went to a local community college and took their science placement test and passed. I enrolled in their cellular biology course and got an A. This motivated me to keep moving forward. I graduated in 2006 with my associate's degree in nursing (ADN). I then pursued a bachelor of science in nursing degree (BSN) in 2008 and master's of science in nursing degree (MSN) / family nurse practitioner in 2012, graduating with honors in all programs. To God be all the glory! This was a confidence booster, and it gave me *courage* to keep pressing on and to not listen anymore to the enemy telling me I was a failure.

You see, the enemy knows the power that an unwavering, steadfast believer has. The Bible says, "I have given you authority to trample on snakes and scorpions and to overcome all the power of the enemy; nothing will harm you" (Luke 10:19). If we learn to walk in this authority, the enemy loses all controlling power over us. For it is in the mind where the battle lies. We have to get mad at the devil and take back what he has stolen from us.

As I deepened my walk with Jesus, I started realizing that I needed to stop living in the past and start living in the present with joyous anticipation of the future, for my best was yet to come! We are more than conquerors through Christ Jesus; we have His strength to help us overcome difficult seasons in life.

Ephesians 6 tells us how to stand against the devil's schemes. We have to *put on* the armor of God daily.

> Stand firm then, with the belt of truth buckled around your waist, with the breastplate of righteousness in

place, and with your feet fitted with the readiness that comes from the gospel of peace. In addition to all this, take up the shield of faith, with which you can extinguish all the flaming arrows of the evil one. Take the helmet of salvation and the sword of the Spirit, which is the word of God. (Ephesians 6:14–17)

See, if we resist the devil, he must flee! (See James 4:7.)

I had to practice over and over thinking on good things and not always looking at situations with a negative mind-set. The Bible says to think on "whatever is true, whatever is noble, whatever is right, whatever is pure, whatever is lovely, whatever is admirable—if anything is excellent or praiseworthy—think about such things" (see Philippians 4:8). Therefore, we have to consciously think on these things to drown out the voice of the enemy who is constantly battling our minds. For he knows that he can dominate us there if we allow him to.

Perfect peace is a gift from God, and the enemy knows that if he can cause confusion or frustration, we will not have peace. Isaiah 26:3 says, "You will keep in perfect peace those whose minds are steadfast, because they trust in you." Steadfast means to be firm in your belief, no matter how you feel or what you see going on around you. It is having full confidence that God will come through in the situation, no matter what.

One of the things I did to help me renew my mind was establish a prayer closet, a place where I could go by myself and spend time with the Lord. I wrote out scriptures and taped them to the wall and listed people I was praying for, as well as prayer requests. This became a kind of a sanctuary for me, a safe haven where I strongly felt the presence of God. I placed posted notes on my mirror displaying uplifting and positive scriptures that counteracted fear to constantly remind me of a new way of thinking. The old programmed mind was being made new. I was learning to see life through a new lens, one of hope and a positive future.

One of my favorite scriptures that I often prayed over my children when they were younger is Jeremiah 29:11, "'For I know the plans I have for you,' declares the Lord, 'plans to prosper you and not harm you, plans to give you hope and a future.'" This type of hope was lacking for so many years in my life. Only by growing my relationship with Jesus have I been able to have hope on this level. God desires to give us a wonderful life, one full of love, peace, and joy. We just have to trust Him!

When my oldest granddaughter was four, she fell outside and scraped her knee. Through her tears, she asked me to pray for it. She said with total assurance, "Jesus will make it better." I studied her face and saw how she fully believed the words she spoke. She did not waver in her belief. She did not question it or ask for proof. She just believed! Recently, my three-year-old granddaughter was playing with her uncle. He asked her to run and jump into his arms. He told her, "I will catch you." At first, I saw hesitation in her little eyes. However, the uncertainty only lasted a few seconds before she took a leap of faith and jumped into his arms, trusting that he would catch her. He did what he assured her he would do. Trust was developed. This is exactly how our heavenly Father wants us to trust Him, with unwavering, childlike faith, a faith I had to learn to develop as an adult. For if I looked at the things through adult eyes and not the eyes of a child, then uncertainty set in, causing me to try to figure things out myself before taking a step. This often resulted in frustration and anxiety.

When I was forty years old, the Holy Spirit impressed on my heart that my inner child would emulate Christ to me. I remember

COURAGE THROUGH THE DARKNESS

thinking that I must have heard incorrectly since the "adult me" would emulate Christ to my "inner child." However, I now understand that it is only through childlike faith that I can I trust the Lord on the level He wants me to. Jesus said, "Truly I tell you, unless you change and become like little children, you will never enter the kingdom of heaven. Therefore, whoever take the lowly position of this child is the greatest in the kingdom of heaven" (Matthew 18:3–4). Going to the Lord with childlike faith allows us to keep our pride in check. This prevents us from striving to exalt ourselves and do things in our own strength. Therefore, to fulfill our calling, one must cast aside arrogance and pride. It allows God to strip us of any qualities that are not pleasing to Him. He needed me to understand this to effectively be set free.

God knows how important family is to me. I have been blessed with such an amazing and supportive family, and it keeps growing! Being a grandmother is the absolute best. The strong emotion I felt the first time I held my child's child is something I will always cherish and remember. I look at my grandchildren with a different view than I looked at my children. I do not believe I fully enjoyed raising my sons on the level that God designed for a mother to. I was so unhealed at the time that I could not see the beauty of childhood. Only through healing have I been able to see the innocence and carefreeness of having a childlike faith through my grandchildren. I get to see it in action! I see pure joy and happiness through their little eyes, much like God created. To trust that all will be well, because mom or dad said so, and even more, because our heavenly Father said so, for He is all knowing, all protecting, all loving! Oh, how freeing that is! Grace prevails!

I have grown abundantly over the years. While most days, my faith now supersedes my fear, I am still a work in progress. But now I have the freedom to express myself, the freedom to love, and the freedom to forgive. While I still struggle at times, like we all do, I don't stay down. I have learned to get up, dust off, and try again.

I look at my past and realize that only God could have pulled me through. I read something recently that said, "God has already prepared the way. He is just preparing you" (author unknown). His incredible love gently encouraged me to persevere through the darkness even when I could not see the path. I had to learn to listen to the still, small voice that spoke ever so gently to my heart. It was only then that I felt a peace. There is richness in adversity and pain since it allows one to grow stronger. I consider it an invaluable gift to be where I am today. I was given a second chance, and I took it. I grabbed hold of Jesus's garment and never looked back. I am so very grateful for every step on my journey that has brought me to this place in my life. I now love deeply and forgive quickly. I find joy in the simplest of things. I accept my emotions and no longer bury them. When I am upset or angry over something, the Holy Spirit whispers in my ear, reminding me to *choose* to forgive. While our flesh wants to take control, we must strive to let our spirit prevail!

Bestselling Christian author Stormie Omartian once said, "In the darkest times of your life, your praise to God should be the loudest. Let the enemy know you're not afraid of the dark."[1] This is something I strive to do daily, to let my praise drown out the voice of the enemy. To stand firm and shout to the rooftops that I am whole and healed in Jesus's name. That darkness no longer controls me. That I am a new creature in Christ. That I am valued and loved deeply by the one who created me, the one who found me worthy to be born, for I have a purpose and I matter. That I am not a mistake. That my best days are yet to come. For I have the promise of heaven and all its glory.

As I have emotionally healed over the years, I look at life differently now. I see the beauty and newness of each day, for each day is a gift. I strive to not let my bad days overwhelm and consume me. Instead, I try to identify something good in them, trusting that God will bring forth a brighter day. I am accepting that my days will not always be on the mountaintop, that valley days will come, but I am not alone when they do. The Reverend Billy Graham once said, "Mountaintops are for views and inspiration, but fruit is grown in the valleys."[2] Growing is hard work and downright painful but necessary if change is to come forth. I had to stop fighting what I could not control and trust the one who did. I was able to face the darkness and allow healing to come forth *only* once I invited Jesus into my life. All along, Jesus was the missing link. He is the beacon of light my life so desperately needed, the light that guided me through the darkness.

It is now time to surrender my fight to the Lord, to give the battle to Him, for it is not mine to fight anymore. This is what true freedom looks like. It is looking through the lens of faith instead of the lens of fear. It is reprogramming a broken, carnal mind to think more Christlike. It is trusting Jesus no matter what the situation looks like. It is having courage to push through the darkness to come out whole on the other side!

My life's motto is "It's not how we start but how we finish. I choose to finish strong!"

However, I consider my life worth nothing to me; my only aim is to finish the race and complete the task the Lord Jesus has given me—the task of testifying to the good news of God's grace.
—Acts 20:24

Do you have a personal relationship with Jesus Christ?

Are you ready to commit your life to Jesus Christ? God is ready and waiting for you. He loves you and created you for a specific purpose, and He has a plan for your life.

The good news is that God accepts us as we are. He does not demand that we come to Him only when we are clean and when our life is all together. Instead, He runs to us with open arms, accepting us completely, filth and all, much like the father did the prodigal son. We do not have to earn salvation, for we are saved by grace. God's love and grace cover a multitude of sins. He just needs us to take the first step and invite Him into our hearts. If you are ready to take this step of faith and commit your life to Jesus Christ, you just need to ask and pray the sinner's prayer:

> Dear God, I know I am a sinner in need of a savior.
> I come humbly to you and ask for forgiveness of
> my sins. I believe Jesus Christ is your son and that
> He died on the cross for my sins, and I believe you
> raised Him from the dead. Please come into my

heart and help me on my new path of righteousness. Guide my life from this day forward. I pray this in the name of Jesus. Amen.

It is that simple! God loves you so very much and only wants the best for you. Now that you have received Him into your heart, it is time to build a strong, intimate relationship with Him. This comes through reading the Bible and fellowship with other believers. Therefore, it is important to surround yourself with others in like faith who will encourage you and lift you up. Please find a good local church to attend and spend time daily in the Word of God, for this is where your faith will grow the most. I am so very proud of the decision you have made today! I pray my story has ministered and touched your heart in some way. I would love to hear from you. Please visit my website at www.cynthiathomas.faith or email me at info@cynthiathomas.faith.

My Blessed Life Now

Notes

Chapter 3. Perseverance through Pain

1   "Bridge over Troubled Water," Simon & Garfunkel, www.simonandgarfunkel.com/music/bridge-over-troubled-water.

Chapter 4. Finding Courage

1   "Courage," Lexico, Accessed February 19, 2020. https://www.lexico.com/en/definition/courage
2   "John Wayne Quotes," Chartcons, www.chartcons.com/famous-john-wayne-quotes.

Chapter 6. Receiving Grace

1   Lewis Sperry Chafer, *Grace* (Findlay, OH: Dunham Publishing Company, 1922), 4.

Chapter 7. Virtuous Woman

1 Rae Simons, *Secrets of the Proverbs 31 Woman* (Uhrichsville, OH: Barbour Publishing, 2015).

2 James Dobson, "7 Ways Dads Influence Their Daughters," https://drjamesdobson.org/blogs/dr-dobson-blog/dr-dobson -blog/2019/07/16/7-ways-dads-influence-their-daughters.

3 James Dobson, "7 Ways Dads Influence Their Daughters," https://drjamesdobson.org/blogs/dr-dobson-blog/dr-dobson-blog/2019/07/16/7-ways-dads-influence-their-daughters.

4 "Teacup story," Just Between Us, https://justbetweenus.org/faith/inspirational-stories/the-teacup-story/.

5 Matthew Henry, *Concise Commentary on the Whole Bible* (Chicago, IL: Moody Press, 1982), 486.

Chapter 8. Pursuing Strength

1 Joyce Meyer, *Be Anxious for Nothing: The Art of Casting Your Cares and Resting in God* (Tulsa, OK: Harrison House, Inc, 1998).

2 Matthew Henry, *Concise Commentary on the Whole Bible* (Chicago, IL: Moody Press, 1982), 486.

3 "Leslie Gould Quotes," Goodreads, https://www.goodreads.com/author/quotes/151399.Leslie_Gould.

Chapter 9. Learning to Forgive

1 "50 Best Quotes to Remind You that Forgiveness Makes you Stronger," Author unknown, Your Tango, https://www.yourtango.com/2018310896/inspirational-forgiveness -quotes-set-your-soul-free-move-on.

Chapter 10. Finding Freedom

1   "Stormie Omartian Quotes," Goodreads,
    https://www.goodreads.com/author/quotes/11785.Stormie_Omartian.

2   "Billy Graham Quotes," Azquotes, https://www.azquotes.com/author/5776
    -Billy_Graham.

Printed in the United States
By Bookmasters